Then the daughters of Zelophehad, the son of Hepher, the son of Gilead, the son of Machir, the son of Manasseh, of the families of Manasseh the son of Joseph, came forward; and these are the names of his daughters: Mahlah, Noah, Hoglah, Milcah, and Tirzah. They stood before Moses, before Eleazar the priest, before the leaders, and all the congregation at the entrance of the tent of meeting, saying, "Our father died in the wilderness, yet he was not among the group of those who gathered together against the LORD, in the group of Korah; but he died in his own sin, and he had no sons. Why should the name of our father be withdrawn from among his family simply because he had no son? Give us property among our father's brothers." So Moses brought their case before the LORD.

Then the LORD said to Moses, "The daughters of Zelophehad are right about their statements. You shall certainly give them hereditary property among their father's brothers, and you shall transfer the inheritance of their father to them."

—Numbers 27:1–7 (NASB)

Extraordinary Women OF THE BIBLE

Extraordinary Women OF THE BIBLE

THE SHADOW'S SONG

MAHLAH AND NO'AH'S STORY

Roseanna M. White

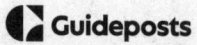 Guideposts

Extraordinary Women OF THE BIBLE

THE SHADOW'S SONG

MAHLAH AND NO'AH'S STORY

DEDICATION

To Xoë—parts of you are in each of these sisters.
I'm so proud of the young woman you've become.

Cast of
CHARACTERS

Abiram • the youngest of Zelophehad's brothers

Cozbi • cousin from the tribe of Manasseh, wishes to marry Mahlah

Danijel • a cousin from the tribe of Manasseh

Gameliel • one of the brothers of Zelophehad

Gila • adopted into the tribe of Benjamin, mother of Uriel

Hoglah • third daughter of Zelophehad

Izik • younger son of Seth, first cousin of the sisters

Kapriel • elder son of Seth, first cousin of the sisters

Keturah • wife of Abiram and sister of the girls' mother

Mahlah • eldest daughter of Zelophehad

Milcah • fourth daughter of Zelophehad

No'ah • second daughter of Zelophehad

Seth • the brother of Zelophehad closest to him in age, father of Kapriel and Izik

Simon • an elder of the tribe of Manasseh

Tirzah • fifth daughter of Zelophehad

Uriel • friend of Kapriel, of the tribe of Benjamin

Zelophehad • of the tribe of Manasseh, had only daughters

CHAPTER ONE

The sweet sound of her sisters' voices raised in song brought a smile to Mahlah's lips and made her fingers itch for her harp. They brushed against manna instead of the familiar strings, gathering the morning's miracle into her bowl. She hummed along with the familiar psalm, though her own voice wasn't as sweet.

A few steps away, No'ah lifted her own voice in praise too, adding a twirl that sent some of the manna out of her own bowl and back to the ground.

Mahlah bit her lip against an instinctual chide. No'ah wasn't a child anymore, to need correction. If she wanted to drop her provisions, laugh, and scoop them again as the cost of her movements, she could.

None of them were children anymore. Mahlah glanced back toward their family's tent—the only home she and her four sisters had ever known—and could imagine them each about their tasks, even though she couldn't see them through the thick fabric. While she and No'ah gathered the manna for the day, Hoglah would be stirring the fire, no doubt dancing around it much like No'ah, though with more grace. Milcah would be tidying up each out-of-place cushion and mat and bowl, determined to make their space as perfect as she could.

And Tirzah, the youngest of her sisters, would be helping *Abba* with whatever he needed for his own tasks and making him smile and laugh in the process.

The song ended, and Mahlah listened to see which one they would take up next—but laughter shrieked out from the tent instead. She chuckled too, without even knowing what the joke was, and scooped up a bit more manna. By rote—or Abba's training, anyway—she scanned the horizon each time she moved, looking for anything that would disturb their peace.

She hadn't brought her harp out with her, but she had the other string she knew so well—her bow, slung always over her arm whenever she set foot outside the camp, just as No'ah had always her twin blades strapped to her sides.

No'ah's pace slowed a moment later, and she straightened, lifting a hand to shield her eyes. Mahlah turned to see what had grabbed her sister's attention, all her mirth fading away when she saw the procession making its way out of the camp, toward the wilderness. Her muscles tensed, ready to reach for bow and arrows if necessary…but no. It was only a funeral procession. Another one. Would it be another victim of the plague that had just swept through the camp to cleanse it of pagan worshipers, or someone who had simply reached the natural end of life?

Given the Midianite women being pulled, weeping, behind the mourners, their sacks of possessions on their backs, she had to assume the first.

No'ah moved closer to her, her gaze fixed on the procession. "How many is that now that we've seen?"

Mahlah shrugged. She'd lost count two days ago, when the plague was at its height. "I still can't believe so many of our young men had taken pagan wives. Are there not enough daughters of Israel for them to choose from?"

No'ah snorted a laugh. "There certainly are now that *we* can all marry."

Though laughter tickled Mahlah's throat again, she shook her head. "Far more than five men were struck down in that plague." And far more than five Midianite women had been ousted from the camp in the last week.

No'ah waved off that obvious truth. "But it was out of frustration at Abba's refusal to entertain suitors, surely, that they looked elsewhere." Her sister sent her a mischievous wink. "But no more."

"No more indeed." Mahlah watched the procession for another moment, long enough to see the family of the dead man shove the pagan women away, long enough to see the two of them spit at the mourners and stomp off in the direction of Shittim. Something strange stirred in her chest. Partly pity, perhaps—she could only imagine the horror those girls felt, and the confusion. They didn't understand what they'd done wrong, what had happened, why their new husbands had been killed by the Lord Himself. They knew only that they'd left their own homes and families, that they'd been prepared to follow their bridegrooms into the Promised Land. And now, this. Sent home in disgrace.

Would they feel guilt? Shame? Or just anger and bitterness?

Mahlah drew in a long breath, the familiar sweet scent of the manna doing little to settle her heart just now. There was pity there, yes. But sorrow too. Sorrow that so many of her people hadn't understood the consequences of their actions. Moses had warned them not to take wives from the lands they crossed through. He'd warned them that no foreign idols were to be brought into the camp—and of course, that's what those women did. That was why their husbands were punished by death straight from God.

No'ah stepped in front of her, her expression crossing a frown with an exasperated sigh. "Are you *crying*? For those women?"

"What?" Mahlah lifted a hand to her cheek, ready to deny the accusation, only to find teardrops there. She breathed a laugh at herself. "It isn't exactly for them. It's for...everything. Everyone. So many men dead, so many women banished back to Shittim, all for a lack of understanding."

Her sister looked at her as though she were half crazed. "It isn't ignorance, Mahlah. It's willful disobedience."

"But only because they don't *understand*." They couldn't. If they did, if they understood the glory of the Lord, how could they possibly turn their backs on Him, on His precepts?

No'ah rolled her eyes and pivoted, but she was smiling again. "Is there ever anyone you don't want to believe the best of?"

"Aren't you glad I always believe the best of *you*?" She couldn't resist a quick tickle to her sister's side. No'ah wasn't quite two years younger than Mahlah, but she'd never had the sort of personality that begged for responsibility to care for the younger girls. It had all fallen to Mahlah when their mother died giving birth to Tirzah.

She'd only been eight. But she'd done all she could for her sisters. She'd learned how to bake the manna into bread, she'd been the one to rock the tearful little ones to sleep, she'd kissed scraped knees and soothed bruised hearts.

Her sisters were more than her sisters. They were her world. She couldn't imagine leaving them—and had insisted she wouldn't, not until they were all prepared to make their own homes with husbands. The clan hadn't understood Abba's willingness to agree with her demand to remain in his tent. After all, it was odd to keep his daughters at home so long, when Mahlah had been of marriable age for so many years already.

But no one argued with Abba. He ducked out of their tent now, his very image the explanation for *why* no one dared to argue with him. He stood a full head taller than any other man in camp, his breadth as intimidating as his height and every inch of it solid muscle. Zelophehad struck the shadow of fear into the hearts of any opponent he faced, which was why most people now just called him the Shadow.

Zelophehad, the mighty warrior. Zelophehad, the fifth of ten mighty sons of Hepher. Zelophehad, respected father of the tribe. Zelophehad, who couldn't help but command respect with his every gaze.

Zelophehad, who was as soft and tender on the inside when it came to his daughters as he was tough as bronze on the outside. He smiled when he spotted them—after examining their sides and making sure they had their preferred weapons within reach—and moved in their direction. Mahlah's chest went a little tighter as she watched him come.

Having only daughters, he'd taken great care to equip them for the world. But they'd taken just as much care to see that his home was one he could be proud of. What would Abba do if they all married and left his tent? Who would care for him? Fix his meals? Tend the womanly chores?

If she voiced *that* concern, she knew he'd get that stern look on his face and say she would not sacrifice her own future happiness, the chance for a family of her own, for him. She would marry now that they were all grown, he would say. And what's more, she would marry someone she loved every bit as much as he still loved her mother.

That part of the conversation, she'd heard often enough that she knew exactly what look would be in his eyes as he proclaimed it. Another dictate that their clan, and even their uncles, didn't understand but didn't dare to question.

"Love will come," their uncle Abiram had tried to say no fewer than a half-dozen times in her hearing alone. He was the youngest of Abba's brothers, but the bond with him was doubly strong because he had married *Imma*'s younger sister. "Choose the best men for them and then trust that the rest will follow, as it always does."

Abba had always shaken his head at Abiram. "It doesn't always. No. No, I want our girls to have what we had. To know that they are treasured and loved and understood. They deserve that."

No one agreed. But it was Abba—so no one argued.

Mahlah had, up until a few months ago, intended to tell her father that she *wanted* him to choose her future husband for her, that she trusted him that implicitly. Which she did. But that was before she'd met Uriel.

"Morning, girls." Abba drew near enough now that she could see he had a large knapsack on his back, a few familiar lengths of tapestry and carved wood poking out. He'd been wanting to venture to Shittim to trade some of their creations for weeks now but had thought it too risky during the height of the plague.

No'ah obviously spotted his purpose too. She rushed toward him, nearly dropping her bowl of manna. "Abba! You're not leaving without us, are you?"

Abba sighed, an exasperated look on his face that didn't fool them for a moment, not given the twinkle in his eye. "You'll slow me down."

"And who wants to rush anyway, on a day as fine as this one?" Grinning, No'ah looked up at their towering father without a shred of doubt in her expression.

Mahlah grinned too and moved at a slower pace toward them. "We can be ready soon. We just need to make a few manna cakes for the trip."

Abba sighed, but it was no more convincing than his scowl. He'd need to eat today too, after all. "Since you'll give me no peace until I agree, very well." Then he winked at them, his grin flashing. "I'll wait for you at the boulder outside camp. I was hoping for a few minutes of quiet prayer before we go."

His plan all along then, no doubt. Mahlah and No'ah both promised to meet him there as quickly as they could manage and hurried back into the tent.

Hoglah had the fire going, ready for the manna they brought her, and she baked the cakes for them while Mahlah and No'ah prepared for the five-mile walk to the city of Shittim. A bit of a thrill warmed Mahlah's blood as she tied her sandals more securely and took the time she hadn't before to rebraid her waist-length hair. Over the years, they'd gone with their father into the cities they'd passed by a few times, to trade or explore. This would be only her third visit to Shittim since they made camp here a year ago, though. Abba didn't like any of them going into the pagan stronghold often.

She didn't *want* to go often—but occasionally, yes. There was an energy to the marketplace that she experienced nowhere else. Something about hearing the various dialects of the region from all the traders and travelers, seeing the varieties of colors, smelling foreign spices from the boggling assortment of foods.

Someday, when they entered the Promised Land and took possession of the cities the Lord had granted them, when they ate the fruit of the land and established their own trade with other countries and cities, this might be commonplace. But it certainly wasn't yet.

A moment's thought convinced her to reach for her knife instead of her bow for this trip. She wasn't as good with it, but it would be easier to conceal in the streets of the city. And besides, they'd have Abba with them. The chances of actually needing protection were slim.

Hoglah spun her way into the partition of the tent that Mahlah and No'ah shared, a smile on her lips. "I have your food ready for you, and Milcah is filling the waterskins for you. Do you need anything else?"

"Not that I can think of. Did you want to come?"

Hoglah wrinkled her nose. "Into the busy, stinking streets of Shittim? No, thank you. I wanted to go with the cousins to check on the sheep in the far pasture. And Milcah and Tirzah already had plans with Sarah today."

Mahlah smiled and leaned over to give the middle sister a kiss on the cheek. "Well then, thank you for helping us get ready, and I'll bring you back something special."

"If you can find more of that cinnamon, I wouldn't argue."

Only Hoglah would ask for spices as a gift. But since they would all enjoy whatever she made with it, Mahlah simply laughed and agreed.

Soon she and No'ah were hurrying back out of the tent, their own small bags with food and water on their backs, their smaller weapons concealed in the folds of their garments, and the angle of the sun telling Mahlah they hadn't gotten ready as quickly as they'd promised. But Abba wouldn't actually mind. He would be lost in prayer anyway, his eyes closed and face lifted to heaven, perhaps a psalm rumbling from his mouth in the rich bass tones she always loved hearing.

"And a good morning to the beautiful daughters of the Shadow."

The voice made Mahlah's every muscle go tense, and she had to fight to keep the pleasant expression on her face as the man stepped into their path. She didn't know what it was about Cozbi that made her react so, exactly. Just that she did, every time he came near. Which was far too often for her peace of mind, especially now that Abba had declared his daughters were ready to wed.

Maybe it was the way his gaze tracked over her from head to toe, as if he were trying to see more than her tunic revealed. Maybe it was the way he was always out here ready to waylay them rather than busy at work as he should have been. Or maybe it was the fact that anytime she did speak to him, he found some way to correct her.

"Good morning, Cozbi," she made herself say, though she also directed No'ah to step around him rather than stop. "Do excuse us—Abba is expecting us."

"He won't mind if you take a moment to exchange a proper greeting."

There, like that. He always did that, or something like it. Anything she said, he had to argue. "We are already later than promised."

"And we have a long day ahead of us too," No'ah added. "We're finally taking some of our goods to trade."

When Cozbi glanced at No'ah, his lip curled up just a bit. Which, come to think of it, was another reason she didn't like him—he didn't like her sister. He sent the same too-sweeping gazes over Milcah that he did Mahlah, though, which made her every bit as uncomfortable on her sister's behalf as when she was the object of his attention.

She picked up her pace. "Have a good day, Cozbi."

"Where are you meeting your father? I'll walk you."

"Wonderful," a new voice said from behind them. "Always happy to have another friend join us. Isn't that right, Uriel?"

Mahlah barely kept from spinning around—if not at Kapriel's voice, than at Uriel's name. Kapriel was her first cousin, but more that than, his father was closest to Abba in age and his best friend, so they'd grown up more like siblings. Kap was one of *her* best friends, and she was always happy to see him.

And she was even happier when he brought his handsome new friend with him, she had to admit. Silently. She'd yet to breathe a word of the flutters in her stomach even to No'ah—though Abba had caught her admiring Uriel last week and had sent her a knowing, twinkling wink that seemed to say, *I see you're considering your options, my song.*

Kap was grinning, his face a convincing mask of welcome as he strode to Mahlah's side, but she knew very well that he didn't like Cozbi any more than she did.

And the feeling was mutual. Upon spotting Kapriel, Uriel, and Kapriel's younger brother Izik, Cozbi's sneer went from a hint to a blow. "Kapriel. I thought you were off hunting today."

Kapriel lifted the bow in his hand. "Indeed. Hence why we volunteered to accompany Mahlah and No'ah to the Shadow, since we apparently can't convince them to join us today."

She could practically see the calculations being done in Cozbi's mind—the chance to walk with them and perhaps even ingratiate himself a bit with their father by doing so, weighed against this additional company he didn't like, and whose presence would likely keep Abba from paying him any mind at all.

Cozbi took a step back toward his tent. "Ah, then my presence would be superfluous. So long as the ladies are protected until they find their father—that was my only concern."

As if *he* would really offer any protection. Mahlah was just as tall as Cozbi and better with a knife, let alone a bow. It was all she could do not to roll her eyes at him.

She tried to catch a glimpse of Uriel without turning her head. He stood half a step behind her cousin, though, making it difficult. She could see only the tip of his nose and a curl of his hair, the morning sun lighting the warm brown with red. Even that sliver of a view was enough to make her heart race.

Then Cozbi ruined it all with another smile that seemed to presume too much. "I'll look forward to visiting with you later though, Mahlah."

She muttered something that she hoped was polite but vague and let her sister pull her back into blessed motion, away from him.

No'ah was breathing a quiet laugh, leaning in close to say, "Could he be any more obvious?"

A shiver coursed through Mahlah. He was a fellow tribesman, a fine prospect for one of them if one were only looking at a list of his attributes and accomplishments and family. But none of those things could counter the fact that she didn't like him.

Feeling someone close ranks on her other side, she glanced up, straight into Kapriel's knowing smile. His dark eyes twinkled and gleamed much like Abba's always did. "I believe you owe me a thank-you."

Laughter bubbled up, now that they were far enough away from Cozbi that she knew he wouldn't hear her. "I most assuredly do. All of you." It gave her an excuse to move her gaze to Izik...and then to Uriel.

He was a Benjaminite, which meant that his family camped in a section of land adjacent to the tents of Manasseh. Even so, she couldn't recall ever having seen him before this last half year. He and Kapriel struck up a friendship when they met up outside the camp, hunting. Not surprising, she supposed, given that the two half tribes of Joseph and the tribe of Benjamin—the three on the west side of the Tent of Meeting— had more than a hundred fifty thousand people between them. There were many people even among her own tribe that she'd never met.

She couldn't say exactly what it was that captured her attention when he was near. Perhaps in part it was his features, his form, the curl to his hair. The way dimples creased his cheeks when he smiled. Or perhaps it was the light in his eyes whenever he spoke, or the way he laughed free and bright at each one of Kapriel's horrible jokes. The way he treated all of her sisters with respect. Maybe it was the way she caught him sneaking glances at her when she was sneaking them at him, clearly not minding overmuch that she stood as tall as most of the men in camp and that her father had trained his daughters more like sons.

Whatever it was, she made no objection when No'ah fell into step with Izik, as she always did, and Mahlah somehow ended up between Kapriel and Uriel. She was just a hair shorter than Uriel—something she always found herself checking against every man she met. Outside her father's father, it was rare that she found anyone taller. Kap had the family height, of course—he topped her by several inches.

She'd always thought she'd want a husband who was taller than she was, tall enough to make her feel safe and protected… but she found herself liking how near she was in height to Uriel. It made it easy to glance over as they spoke of their hopes for the morning's hunt, to exchange a smile with him.

They'd only spoken a few times when it was just the two of them. Enough to make her long for another few moments of comparative solitude with him, for the chance to get to know him better, to ask him the things that Kap never would.

Was he eager for the last leg of their journey into the Promised Land? Did his soul yearn to learn more of Lord, like hers did? Like Abba's? What dreams did he have for the future, when their generation settled the land and ate of the milk and honey God had sworn would be theirs?

A thrill warmed her heart whenever she considered it. The murmurs around the camp were that it wouldn't be long now—that this plague God had sent upon them was to purge the ranks of any whose heart had strayed from Him, so that a pure and holy people would be ready to make the final march into what the last generation had failed to seek.

She was ready. Whenever her eyes cast toward Canaan, her pulse quickened and her stomach went tight in anticipation. All her life, their people had been wanderers, moving from one camp to another, waiting for the faithless generation to pass away. She had eaten manna every day, and that steady diet of the miraculous had made her hungry for the fulfillment of *all* the Lord had promised them. She wanted to eat of the fruit of a land that was their own. She wanted to experience walls of stone or brick around her when she awoke. She wanted to raise a family knowing that those children and their children would be on the same piece of land long after she'd passed from the earth.

"You look lost in thought, Mahlah."

She felt heat rush to her cheeks at Uriel's soft words, but she shook off the contemplation and smiled. "Just dreaming of when Moses and Joshua take us into the Promised Land."

He chuckled, those dimples flashing. "You're looking much further ahead than I am. I find myself dreaming rather happily about…now. Or the next month or two."

Something about the way he said it, the way he looked at her as he did, made her cheeks warm even more. Did he mean he dreamt of getting to know her? It felt as if he did, and the way his gaze caught hers and lingered there, the way his smile broadened and yet seemed to point only at her, seemed to corroborate the suspicion.

"I…" She scarcely knew how to respond. She'd spent so many years raising her sisters and refusing to even consider her own heart that the idea of capturing a man's attention and then doing something with it felt foreign. Even so, it was heady. Her own smile shifted into something half shy and half giddy. "I dream of now too. Of the immediate future."

Uriel slowed his pace under the guise of repositioning his bow, and Mahlah remained at his side, letting Kap drift a few feet ahead of them. He didn't even seem to notice their lagging, given that he was saying something to his brother that had Izik laughing, and No'ah too.

The way Uriel cleared his throat brought her attention back to him. He dropped his voice to a murmur. "Mahlah, I...I mean to speak with your father. Now that you—that is, if you're amenable. I realize we scarcely know each other, but I would cherish the opportunity to remedy that, if..."

Perhaps she'd only known him a short time, but never in that time had she ever heard him stumble over his words as he did now. Gone was the man renowned for his hunting, welcomed into any group, able to speak and joke with anyone. And he'd been reduced to stammering over *her*? That was enough to make her smile shift into a grin.

"I would like that, Uriel. More than I can say."

"Truly?" At her nod, he flashed a deep grin. "You've just made the day brighter."

She was about to say that he'd made hers all the better too, but they'd exited the camp and were approaching the boulder where Abba had said he'd be waiting, and No'ah stole her attention when she shouted, "Abba?"

A word her sister shouted frequently—but never like that. Instead of greeting or welcome or joy, her voice was...Mahlah didn't even know the word. Alarmed? Panicked? Horrified?

Those two syllables, shouted in that tone, were enough to change the racing of her heart from joy at Uriel's intentions to the sickest dread. The last time she'd heard her sister sound like that had been when they were just children. When No'ah had gone in to check on Imma after Tirzah was born and had found her lifeless and still.

Fifteen years hadn't been enough to wipe that memory from her heart. Mahlah shifted away from Uriel so that she could see around Kapriel and Izik, to where No'ah was sprinting toward the boulder. What had she seen? Without conscious thought, her fingers sought the handle of her knife.

"No'ah, wait!" Mahlah cried, rushing forward. Izik reached her in two steps and caught her around the waist with one strong arm, yanking her back.

Mahlah felt the jerking motion, only it pulled her forward, toward them, rather than catching her up short. Kapriel tried to block her path, but she didn't even glance up at his familiar face. She just sidestepped him, moved one more step, and then crumpled to the ground beside her sister and Izik, her throat aching with a scream she wasn't aware of otherwise.

Abba lay on the ground at the base of the boulder, the ground stained red beneath him and a dagger buried in his back up to the hilt.

CHAPTER TWO

No'ah sat in their tent, the ache in her back and tingling in her toes telling her she'd been in the same position too long. She didn't care. Usually she preferred motion to rest, but that was because movement meant life.

Life was gone. It had been stolen by a Midianite dagger. Abba—their strong, fearless, awe-inspiring abba—had been struck down while he was praying, that cursed dagger plunged into his back. His life, gone. *Her* life, gone. What was she, if not second daughter of the Shadow? Who would any of them be now, without Abba?

She wanted to search out each of her sisters in the crowded, busy tent, but she couldn't convince her eyes to shift from the cook fire she'd been staring at for…however long it had been since she'd collapsed here, after Izik practically carried her back from the boulder. She was aware, at least peripherally, of the constant coming and going of friends and family and neighbors. She'd heard the tribe's elders hurry in, after examining Abba's body, to assure Mahlah that they would record his death as being an enemy attack and not a result of the pagan-purging plague—that his reputation would remain pristine.

Reputation. As if his reputation mattered now. As if *anything* mattered.

She heard Tirzah greet their aunt Keturah—Imma's sister, as well as Uncle Abiram's wife—and Abiram and welcome them inside. She heard the horror in each new voice. The pain. The disbelief.

None of them compared to hers and her sisters'. None could. No one who lived outside these tapestry walls could possibly understand the hole that had just opened up beneath them. It wasn't just that they were orphans now—they had uncles and aunts enough to guarantee they'd never be alone if they didn't want to be. It wasn't that they had no protector, no provider—Abba had taught them to protect and provide for themselves. It was that *Abba* was gone—the one who laughed with them, danced with them, doted on them, trained them. The one who insisted each of his daughters was more precious than ten sons, and that each one deserved happiness and love.

That was what rendered her frozen now. Love and life, snuffed out like a lamp without oil, and with that fuel gone, she couldn't convince herself to move.

Milcah settled at her side—No'ah could tell it was her even without looking up, just by the jangle of the anklet she wore and the grace of her movements as she sat. Her little sister scooted close, let out a gust of breath, and rested her cheek on No'ah's shoulder.

Why was *that* the thing that made tears sting her eyes, made her spine bend and her muscles sag? She wrapped an arm around Milcah and turned in to her, pulling her closer. Milcah clung to her too, their mixed tears turning to sobs that left her every bit as achy and tired as sitting so still for so long had done.

"I don't want to do this," Milcah whisper-gasped into No'ah's ear after she'd regained enough of her breath.

No'ah could only nod. She didn't have to ask what her sister meant—it wasn't the funeral, not the burial, not even the prospect of leaving their father behind here in this foreign land when they broke camp. She wouldn't even be talking about managing the household without him. She meant something deeper, more primal: She didn't want to face life without their abba. He had been the axis around which they all rotated for... always.

"I know," No'ah gasped back. "I don't either."

They huddled there together until the fire dried their tears. No'ah was just noticing that her legs were going numb again when Tirzah joined them, which forced her to reposition. Then Hoglah arrived a minute later, her face as tear-streaked as No'ah's must be. Usually if this many people were in their tent, Hoglah would have been here at the cook fire constantly, making this or that and offering it to their guests.

Nothing about today qualified as "usual," other than the manna cakes sitting on their platter.

Having three of her sisters huddled around her inspired No'ah to look beyond the fire, in search of Mahlah. She spotted her by the door flap, looking deep in conversation with Abiram and Keturah. Would they, perhaps, be the ones officially put in charge of them now? As the youngest of her uncles, it wouldn't be the logical choice of guardian—but that double link to them might make it so. Especially since Abiram was always the organizer among the brothers. He'd studied as a scribe and seemed to enjoy keeping accounts like No'ah enjoyed running free through the meadows.

Mahlah stood tall, even though No'ah knew the burden of the whole family had just landed squarely on her older sister's shoulders. Her cheeks were dry, if pale. Her eyes steady, if red-rimmed. The only real indication of the pain she knew Mahlah felt down to her bones was the tremor in her hands, visible even from over here.

Poor Mahlah. She wouldn't let herself crack, wouldn't let herself cry until all the details had been dealt with and all the mourning guests had drifted back to their own tents. She would push on, past her own pain and numbness, as long as a duty remained to be done.

Something stirred inside No'ah, something that said she ought to be standing there beside Mahlah, helping her sort everything out. If she made herself move, though, if she went over there and stood beside her, Mahlah would only nudge her back again. Because Mahlah knew her too well, knew what she needed, and she couldn't help but give each of them whatever that was.

For No'ah, that meant this was a time to be still and silent before throwing herself back into motion and doing any task not yet done by the others. For Hoglah, it meant the requests for food and drink for their guests that she'd already set out. For Milcah, it was the task of making them all look presentable at the funeral tomorrow. For Tirzah, choosing the songs and dirges they would sing over their fallen father.

No'ah and the younger three didn't try to take any of that delegating responsibility from Mahlah—because that was what *she* needed. To maintain what control she could. To tend the rest of them. It would be cruel to deprive her of her one comfort.

A moment later, sunlight spilled into the tent again, mocking in its brightness. How could it still be day? So early, even? How did the sun not turn its face away in grief when Abba fell?

So busy was she glaring at the sun that it took her a long moment to realize that the sudden onslaught was due to the return of Izik, Kapriel, and Uriel. They'd vanished at some point, though the exact moment was a blur. One of them had accompanied her and Mahlah back here...another had fetched the elders...the other had gone for all their uncles and aunts. The majority of their grieving relatives had left along with the elders, but as for their friends...

Well, they were here again now, and the sight of Izik moved something inside much like her sisters had done. He was very nearly as much a part of her life as they were, having been the one she played with as a child, being just her age. If she'd had a brother, she'd have wanted him to be like Izik. And having him made her feel as though she had one in all the ways that mattered.

Except the most important one. The one that would mean he was here, now, to take possession of all that had been Abba's. To take care of the five sisters.

Izik met her gaze the moment he'd finished blinking to adjust to the dimmer interior light, and in the next second he was hastening toward her. Her sisters made room for him, Tirzah simply sinking into his side with a sniff. He slid an arm around her and then put one around No'ah too and squeezed her close. "How are you, No?"

It was a stupid question. He'd know it. But what else was there to ask or to say? No'ah couldn't find any clever rebuttals, but she leaned into his side and sighed. Her gaze, rather than staying focused on his familiar face, had drifted back to the entryway.

Kap and Uriel both hovered there still, near Mahlah and Abiram. It made sense, she supposed. Kapriel and Mahlah were as much friends as she and Izik. Uriel, though, she would have assumed stayed close to Kapriel...except that his eyes were focused on Mahlah, and in a way that spoke of something beyond sympathy.

She blinked, half expecting her eyes to clear and for him to be just one more visitor. Because if he was interested in Mahlah, it wouldn't have just sprung up this moment. But if it had been there for any length of time already, how had she missed it?

Izik rubbed a hand over her arm. "You scare me when you're still like this, No'ah. This isn't how you're supposed to be. I scarcely recognize you when you're not buzzing about."

On a different day, it may have made her smile. He'd long called her a bee, buzzing from one flower to the next. But was that in fact the answer to her unspoken question about Uriel? Had she not paused to really *look*? To observe? To see?

More disturbing still—Mahlah just snuck a glance at Uriel. Mahlah, who was barely clinging to composure. Whose pain was burrowing down deeper with every moment. Whose entire focus since they regained their tent had been taking care of everything she possibly could—*Mahlah* just took a moment of her precious concentration to look at a young man who hadn't even spoken.

A handsome young man. Not the sort that appealed to No'ah, but clearly Mahlah had different preferences.

"Oh." She didn't mean to speak it out loud. Wasn't even sure she would have had this moment when it was all so clear in any other situation. But it was obvious now, as she sat in the stillness. As she looked in a way she never did at any other time. As she saw what *was* rather than what could be if she rushed to catch it. Mahlah and Uriel favored each other...and if Abba were here, he'd insist they explore that, get to know each other, decide if they could build a love to last a lifetime.

But Abba was gone. And Abiram or another of their uncles would be the ones making decisions for them. Their uncles, who had tried time and again to talk Abba out of his odd decisions concerning his daughters. What if they wouldn't honor Abba's wishes? What if they simply arranged marriages for all of them? If they did that, what were the chances that they'd look twice at the near stranger from a different tribe?

No'ah pushed herself up, swaying a bit when her head went light from the action. She was none too sure she wouldn't have just tumbled down again if Izik hadn't stood too and steadied her with a hand on her elbow. "No'ah?" Concern dripped from his voice.

She swallowed and glanced down at her younger sisters. They were better at observation than she was, especially Tirzah. Making sure her voice stayed low, she asked, "How long has Mahlah been looking at Uriel like that?"

For half a second, Tirzah and Milcah both grinned. Then reality set upon them again, and their matching smiles faded into matching frowns. They were quick-witted, both of them.

They'd be tracing the question to its new, horrible conclusions. Tirzah frowned. "Our uncles will allow it, don't you think?"

Milcah had taken her lip between her teeth. "She hasn't breathed a word of it before. But I've been thinking they would soon speak to Ab—" A sob cut her off.

Hoglah wrapped Milcah into a tight embrace. No'ah stroked a hand over her head too, but Abiram was striding back outside. No'ah darted after him.

"No'ah." Izik dogged her heels, of course. "Now isn't the time to talk to him about this."

Now was the *perfect* time. Before he could talk to his brothers about making any plans for them—and they would, they'd see it as their duty. By the time their forty days of mourning were over, Abiram or another of their uncles would have arranged five husbands for the five daughters of his brother. If her uncles ended up in a group of tribal elders, it could well come up this very night. She had to speak to Abiram first. Now. "I have to. Before others can."

Izik huffed out his opinion of that, but he didn't try to forcibly stop her from darting past Mahlah, Kapriel, and Uriel. He simply followed her outside, into the mocking sunlight. Though once they'd cleared the tent, before they'd caught Abiram, he did say, "It will wait until tomorrow. You can take today to grieve what's lost rather than worrying about what's next."

She sidestepped a gaggle of toddlers chasing each other and kept her gaze trained on her uncle. He was moving at a quick pace, with a goal clearly in mind, though she couldn't discern yet what it would be. "If only that were true."

"It *is* true. None of the uncles are going to make any life-altering decisions for you all in the next twelve hours."

She spared her friend a glare. "You don't know that."

He hesitated, lips parted but no quick rebuttal spilling out—all the proof she needed that her instincts here were right. He knew Abiram as well as she did. He knew, just as she did, that her uncle would think the best way to honor Zelophehad would be to see to his daughters' futures as quickly as possible. He could be going even now to talk to the elder brothers and take the responsibility for them onto his own shoulders. His motivation would be good.

That didn't mean they'd like his actions.

He passed through a crowd of milling neighbors, the stricken looks on their faces telling No'ah that it was her father's violent demise occupying them. She nearly lost track of her speeding uncle in the murmuring mass—a problem she'd never once had with Abba, who stood so much taller than everyone else.

Such a silly thing to nearly double her over in fresh pain. Never again would she see his head bobbing above the others in a crowd. Never again would she watch his expression flash from serious and somber with his neighbors to mischievously delighted at spotting his daughters.

Never again would she hear his laugh boom out across the distance and straight into her heart.

She ought to have just called out to her uncle the moment she stepped out of the tent. If she tried it now, he wasn't likely to hear her over the general din of camp. Why had that not even occurred to her? She mumbled the question to Izik.

He chuckled. "Because you'd rather run than shout, Little Bee."

She could hardly argue with that. And the clan was so accustomed to seeing her do so that no one looked twice now when she broke from a fast walk into an outright run to try to catch up with her long-legged uncle. Why had she inherited Imma's petite stature instead of Abba's height, like Mahlah and Milcah had done?

Eventually, a neighbor spotted both her and Abiram and sorted out the problem. "Abiram!" Jehoakim shouted. "Wait up for your niece!"

He paused, spun around, a startled look on his face. When he spotted her, it turned to a confused frown. "No'ah," he said in greeting when she'd drawn near enough to hear him. "Did Mahlah send you after me? Is something the matter? I mean, something other than…"

"I hope not." At least she had no need to catch her breath after such a short run. Logic said that perhaps she should try a smile, but her lips refused to cooperate. "Mahlah didn't send me." Her older sister would have known where Abiram was going though, of course. She'd likely been the one to send him out on whatever errand he was about.

Abiram glanced at Izik, as if expecting him to make sense of No'ah actions, but Iz had never been one to try to explain her "buzzing" to anyone else. He just put on that placid not-quite-a-smile he always used to deflect unwanted questions. That expression had somehow managed to keep them both out of trouble more times than she could count. It scattered calm far and wide, though she could never be sure how. A mysterious talent that made him the perfect co-conspirator in all her adventures though.

For now, she simply drew in a deep breath, pushed down the pain that had held her captive, and lifted her chin. "You know our father's desire for us all to marry where our hearts incline."

Abiram's confusion fell away, but incredulity took its place in his eyes. He was a good man, a kind man, but patience—especially with anything he deemed an oddity—had never been his strong suit, and he was already glancing away, clearly eager to be back about his business. "You chased me down to talk about your future marriages mere hours after your father was slain?"

The words made her wince. The implied accusation made her take a step back. But that, in turn, made her bump into Izik, and the reminder of his presence lent her strength. Rather than lift her chin in defiance, she reached for Abiram's hand. "Not for myself. It's just—Mahlah has already given so much of her life for the rest of us. And now, without Abba..." She had to squeeze her eyes shut to hold back a fresh onslaught of tears. "She deserves every happiness. She deserves to chase what *she* wants for once. And though I know she won't be giving it any thought right now...I need to know she'll have that chance. Now, more than ever."

Abiram drew in a long breath, heaved it out again. "You trust me so little to see to her happiness? You think I won't arrange what's best for her? Kapriel is the obvious choice—"

"I know he is." And if it came down to it, Kap and Mahlah would no doubt build a strong family and make a fine life together. But they were more like siblings than spouses in their affections, just as she and Izik were. She shook her head. "And if you arranged it, neither would argue. But it isn't what they want. She..." Did she dare reveal the secret her sister hadn't breathed a word of to anyone, even her? She swallowed. "I think her heart is inclining elsewhere. Please, Abiram. Give her the chance to discover if it's a love worth pursuing."

Abba had loved all his brothers, but being one of twelve siblings—the ten boys and two daughters besides—meant there were natural pairings and favorites. Izik's father, Seth, had always been closest to him in both age and friendship. But Abiram had become a better friend when he'd married Imma's sister. Though there were eight between them in age, they'd ended up spending a lot of time together after that.

But he and Abba were also so very *different* in so many ways. Where Abba was—had been—a mighty man, always the first to volunteer for a scouting mission, always chosen as a guard for the camp, Abiram was a scribe, spending all his time in tents, with wax tablets and styluses and papyrus, when it was available. Where her father was heart and instinct, Abiram was logic and reason.

She was too much like Abba to ever anticipate what Abiram might say or do.

Abiram didn't just sigh this time, he sagged. In that moment, he looked younger than she usually thought of him, and she realized he was still closer to thirty than to forty—not so much older than Mahlah. His children were still children, chasing their friends and cousins around the camp and years away from things such as marriage contracts. This wasn't a burden he was ready for. Not one he'd ever have asked to take on. Perhaps he was even thinking that he'd just leave this dilemma to the older uncles.

Even if that happened, he'd still be a voice. A respected one. Perhaps he was different from the others with his styluses and tablets, but that very thing meant his older siblings all held him in a certain respect.

"You know I want the best for you," he said, his voice sounding weary and worn. "All of you. We all do."

"I know." She gave his fingers a squeeze. "And I know it isn't fair that all this has landed on one of you, but…" Tears choked her voice, and she had to pause and swallow to clear them. "She'd never ask this herself. You know she wouldn't. And I'm not asking it for me—arrange whatever you like, if that's what you want to do. But Mahlah…honor Abba's wishes for Mahlah."

He squeezed her fingers back and looked deep into her eyes. "You know we can't do that, No'ah. Either we arrange things for all of you, or we let you all choose. We can't just grant that to Mahlah and then tell Tirzah she has no say in the matter." This time, he was the one to wince at his own words. "Not that I would ever make arrangements without your input. I'm no tyrant. I want you to be happy and fulfilled, all of you. But I know that my own parents' wisdom made for a far better match than my own young, fleeting emotions would have led me to."

She probably shouldn't be offended on her aunt's behalf at that—though she wanted to be. Keturah was bright and sweet and lovely. How could his heart ever have wanted him to look elsewhere?

But that was silly. Hearts seldom employed the same logic that minds did. An observation that wouldn't help her point at all. "Perhaps...a compromise? Especially with Mahlah, consider where her heart leans, and then examine any potential husbands with the care I know you and the other uncles will employ. You know she'll welcome your advice and counsel—we all will. But why not entertain possibilities where there is already affection?"

Abiram patted her hand with his free one. "That sounds fair enough. For *all* of you."

She smiled, because she was grateful for Mahlah's sake. For her own...she'd yet to see any one young man who made her want to dance and sing. And she couldn't imagine that changing anytime soon, with this shadow of grief overhanging her.

CHAPTER THREE

Mahlah sat with her sisters, surrounded not only by family but by everyone in Israel who had known her father—which was hundreds, perhaps even thousands of people. The gathering for the funeral had been so big that they'd had to hold it well outside the camp, and every wife in Manasseh had brought a dish of food and was helping to serve it to the crowd, which meant that she had nothing to occupy her hands. Her cousins had created a barrier between the masses and the Shadow's daughters, so there wasn't currently anyone to greet. Her sisters had all purged their tears earlier, so there was no one to soothe.

She'd thought she knew what it felt like to have her insides carved out and left hollow. That was how she remembered feeling at eight, when Imma died. She recalled holding a little hollowed-out wooden toy that Abba had made her years before and thinking she was just the same. It looked right on the outside, but when you picked it up, it was light as a whisper, because nothing was left inside.

Losing her mother at such a young age had been horrible. But losing Abba now was worse—perhaps because nothing had ever completely filled up that first gaping hole. So when the ravages of this new loss took a knife to her soul again, what could it do but leave even less of her?

She toyed with a piece of manna cake without actually eating it, not sad when she saw some of the more distant crowd was dispersing. The ones that mattered, the ones who truly knew him and them, would stay for hours yet. Campfires were already being lit, and old Simon, one of the tribe's elders, had taken up a seat in the middle of a gaggle of cousins. "I remember when Zelo was just a boy," he was saying, his voice carrying over the wilderness and caressing her heart as much as her ears. "Just a boy but tall as a man! From behind, he looked like any other fighter, until you saw his youthful face. Well, one day we were chasing off a band of raiders, and Zelo snuck into the ranks with his older brothers when no one was looking."

Her lips turned up just a bit at the edges. She'd heard the story before, countless times—Abba's first taste of battle at the age of twelve. He'd not struck the shadow of fear into anyone that time. *He'd* been the one frightened, not by an enemy but by a mountain goat that had come up behind him and started bawling. She chuckled along with everyone else as old Simon described how high Abba jumped in fright, and how it was that squeal that gave him away to his brothers. His father had at first been in a rage that the boy had come along after he'd been forbidden from doing so, but amusement had won out. As it always did with Zelophehad. No one could ever stay angry with him, because his heart was as big as his stature.

From there, someone else took up the storytelling, and then another. She scooted closer to No'ah and Milcah, set the uneaten cake aside, and let the sorrow bend itself into a smile as she listened. Story after story, most of them familiar but a few she'd not heard before, warmed the evening as the sun set. All of them painting an image that equaled Abba.

His bravery but also his humor. The jokester and the warrior. The neighbor always quick to help, the stubborn man who refused to bend an inch when it came to the wife he wanted. The doting abba. The wise leader.

She was aware of Kap easing down beside her at one point, Uriel with him, and she dug up a smile to send them, trusting the firelight would carry it to their eyes. They'd been nothing but supportive this last wretched day, present every moment they possibly could be. Kapriel's father had been Abba's dearest friend, after all, and he was one of the men who had accepted the time of uncleanness in order to care for and bury Zelophehad's body. In Seth's absence from camp, Kapriel had been the one to do everything that his father otherwise would have, and Uriel had scarcely left his side. In part because they'd become such good friends.

In part, she knew from their conversation before everything shattered, because he wanted to spend time with *her*.

There had been no opportunity for a private conversation, of course. But he was there. Supporting her. Helping with whatever he could. Watching her, clearly ready to lend a hand or a supportive arm at any moment.

It was a lot for him to offer, for a man she was only just coming to know. And it meant the world.

Uncle Gameliel's story of Abba startling off a whole band of wanderers single-handedly ended with a roar of laughter, and then a sigh seemed to travel around the congregation collectively too. "Such a legacy he leaves behind him," Abba's second-oldest brother said. He stared into the fire, shaking his head. "Such a shame there's none to carry on his name. No one to take possession of the land that would have been his, when we march on the Promised Land."

It felt as though a coal from the fire took up residence in her chest. All her life, Mahlah had been hearing how sad it was that Imma had given Abba no sons, only daughters. All her life, Abba had been claiming each of his daughters was worth ten sons. And perhaps in his eyes they were.

But Gameliel was right too. There was no one to carry on his name. No one to claim an inheritance for him. No one to make sure he was remembered, though he deserved to be more than most.

"And why not?"

The nearness of the voice made her startle even before the familiarity of it did. Uriel. He didn't stand, but the attention of everyone shifted toward him as his voice rang out through the dusk-painted evening.

"What's that?" Gameliel asked.

Uriel motioned toward them—Mahlah, No'ah, Hoglah, Milcah, and Tirzah. "The Shadow is far from childless. He has five daughters who are no less part of Israel, part of Manasseh, than he was. Why shouldn't *they* carry on his legacy? Inherit the land in his name?"

For a moment, silence descended. For a moment, the whole earth stood still. For a moment, Mahlah could only stare at

Uriel along with everyone else as the impossibility of it hovered all around her.

Of course that couldn't happen. Everyone knew that men inherited, not women. Everyone knew that a woman's job was to become part of her *husband's* family and tribe, not have her own. Everyone knew that she and her sisters could never be to Abba what a son would have been, despite his loving claims and unusual training.

Except that Gameliel jumped to his feet, and it wasn't incredulity on his face. It was…excitement? "You're right." His voice sounded nearly feverish. He turned to Simon. "Isn't he? Why shouldn't the girls inherit in their father's name, when there's no son? It's far more fair than letting the Shadow's legacy die with him."

She expected the elder to shake his head and declare it a notion utterly foolish. But Simon looked contemplative. "He was a man after the Lord's heart," he said, voice musing. "One dedicated fully to his wife and daughters. A man of noble heart and fearless courage, and whose daughters do him honor." He nodded.

And then his gaze arrowed in on *her*. "Mahlah—you will have to go before Moses. All of you! You will have to make an appeal to him, to receive your father's inheritance."

"I…what?" Did her voice even emerge, or was the croak only in her own mind? She might have thought herself dreaming the whole thing, if No'ah weren't shaking her arm.

Simon was smiling now, as was Gameliel, who'd turned and moved through the crowd toward them. "We'll put in the petition on your behalf. Coming from the tribal elders, it will go directly to Moses—he will have to inquire of the Lord. But you can present your case. Show him how deserving you are, and how deserving your father was of being remembered through you."

Mahlah's throat went tight, her stomach cramping. It was on the tip of her tongue to refuse, to say she had no need of land or legacy, no need to bother their leader.

Moses. She'd only ever seen him from a distance, but she didn't have to know the man personally to shudder in awe at the very thought of an audience with him. He was the chosen of God. One of the few men still alive who'd been part of the Exodus from Egypt. The only person since the first father and mother in the garden to see the Lord with his own eyes, hear His voice daily.

He would take one look at her and see her every failing. He'd know that she wasn't deserving of anything. She was just a scared girl who had clung for years to the excuse of caring for her sisters so she wouldn't have to face the deepest fear of her heart: that she'd never have what her parents did, and that she'd leave children of her own behind in a hollowed-out mess someday when something took *her* life too early too.

A fear she'd never looked square in the eyes until now, at the prospect of looking *him* square in the eyes.

"Mahlah!" No'ah's whisper, fervent and bright, brought her gaze back from Gameliel and his frightening offer. She looked at her sister—all her sisters. At the light of hope shining through the cloud of grief. At the way their lips were all parted, at how each of them sat a little straighter at the thought that perhaps they could do something for their father's memory. Perhaps they *could* carry on the legacy they'd been told all their lives was beyond them simply because they were born female.

Mahlah sucked in a long breath. If it were only her, she wouldn't have the courage to do it. Though she looked more like Abba than the others, No'ah had been the one to inherit his boldness, Hoglah his bravery, Milcah his strength, Tirzah his personality. For herself, she would do nothing.

But for them—they deserved everything. Anything.

Unable to make her throat work, Mahlah could only nod.

It was enough.

Uproar erupted, a line of flame and starlight against the dark night of grief. A central fire where the elders talked and planned and laughed, but then sparks going out to the whole assembled crowd of extended family.

Though Mahlah heard them, it felt as though her head were underwater and their voices were muffled by fluid more than distance. She was left more with the impression of conversation than understanding of it.

Is it possible? That was the prevailing theme. *Will Moses allow it? What would that mean?*

A shiver coursed up her spine, which she would have happily blamed on the cool of night, except that between the campfire and the press of her sisters' bodies against hers, she had no hope of even feeling that darkness-chilled breeze. No, the shiver was the same one that had given her father his nickname—the shadow of fear.

It wasn't just her own, *their* own fates she'd be asking Moses to decide, she knew that. He was the great Lawgiver. When he made pronouncements, it wasn't for individuals—it was inspired by individuals, but which created precedent that would become law for *everyone*. For the entire nation, not just her family or tribe. If Moses decided in their favor, it would be then the way it was done for *all* men who died with only daughters.

If he decided against them, it would mean no other daughters could ever petition him.

Beside her, Kapriel reached for her hand and gave her fingers a squeeze. He didn't look over at her, just whispered, "I know it's a burden, Mahl. But it isn't one you'll be carrying alone. Breathe."

Only at his reminder did she realize that all the air had backed up in her lungs and her head had gone light from it. She let it out slowly enough to not gain her sisters' attention and then drew a fresh breath in just as carefully. The dizziness faded, though the weight of responsibility didn't lessen any. Not yet.

Kapriel let her fingers go and faced Uriel, who had positioned himself so that his back was to the fire, his attention focused now on them.

On *her*.

Kapriel chuckled. "I can't believe you actually made that suggestion to the elders, Ur."

There was something so alluring about the contradictions of him—the confidence of his shrug, but the self-deprecating humor in his smile. "They aren't *my* elders," he said, laughter in his voice. "If the suggestion had offended them, it wouldn't have had any great effect on me. I thought it worth the risk of embarrassment if they'd dismissed the idea."

Through the gathering night, his gaze found hers and settled on her face. "You and your sisters deserve to keep everything your father worked for. And he deserves to be honored and remembered. To be counted with his brothers."

The words were sweeter to her spirit than any praise of her beauty could have been, more endearing than a love song. Perhaps she hadn't known Uriel long, but he clearly understood her, to realize what she most needed to hear right now.

"Thank you." The words came out like a ghost through her tight throat, as much not-there as there...quite possibly only in her mind and not real at all.

But no, he smiled a reply. Which meant either she really had made a sound, or he could see the gratitude in her eyes. "You are very welcome, Mahlah." *His* words most certainly emerged, and as a gentle caress that felt as warm and tender as a kiss.

Her cheeks warmed at the comparison in her thoughts. And then her heart ached like someone had just kicked her in the chest.

What was she doing? Dreaming of a man at her father's funeral—how selfish could she be? This wasn't the time for thoughts of romance and embraces, it was the time for remembering her father. Even if the man in question *had* made her think such things by risking censure from her elders by suggesting something to honor him.

And Abba would have thrilled at the suggestion. Had they thought to make the petition while he yet lived, he would have been the one charging forth to the elders to suggest it, guiding them in what to say. He would have had advice on how best to present themselves to him. He would have himself made an impassioned plea for his daughters to inherit.

Would it have gotten past even the elders though? They had always simply replied that he ought to remarry and have more children until a son or two came along. No one had understood why he refused. No one could see how Imma still lived so vibrantly in his heart, in their home, despite having not been alive within the walls for so long.

He saw her still, Mahlah knew. Her stature in No'ah. Her face in Hoglah. Her voice in Milcah. Her laughter in Tirzah. How could he not still love her, when his daughters kept her memory alive in their mere being?

Perhaps, as long as he lived, this petition would never have been made. But if he was aware of anything in the world beyond this one, where he rested in the bosom of Abraham, he would be glad to see them making it now. She knew that.

Just as she knew that if he were somehow here, sitting beside her, he would nudge her attention right back to Uriel and say, *Don't be afraid to feel it, precious one. You deserve happiness, even now. I want you to find what I had with your imma.*

Even now. She could hear the words echoing in that place in her heart that had just throbbed, hear them in Abba's deep voice. She could hear him whispering that he loved her, that she and her sisters were both his weakness and his strength.

She could hear him lifting his voice in praise to the Lord who had given him this life, these children, the wife he'd held too few years. She could hear him worshiping God for all He gave and for all He took away.

Blessed be the name of the Lord.

She didn't realize she'd lifted her own voice in Abba's favorite psalm, not until her sisters joined her in harmony and someone, from somewhere, slipped a harp into her hands. Her fingers found the strings with the ease and familiarity that came of two decades of practice, and her sisters' voices buoyed up her own, strengthening it when she would have wavered off into silence again upon realizing she'd interrupted the conversation.

They sang. That psalm and then another, never pausing to wonder what to sing next. They knew the repertoire as well as they knew how to scoop manna from the ground and turn it into every bread they ever needed. It was the lifeblood of their family, these words of praise and worship and love for the God who had saved them, who had made them, who was preparing even now a place for them.

Words Abba had spoken countless times through the years, as he turned toward the Promised Land.

Words that trembled now in her soul in a whole new way. Was He? Was God preparing a place for *them*? The daughters of Zelophehad? Would He hear their song and honor their father with favor toward them? Would He grant them a future as co-inheritors with their male cousins?

Her fingers danced over the strings, hope warring with wonder that wasn't quite doubt but wasn't quite faith either.

She wasn't Moses—she didn't know the heart of God so well. Perhaps He would see them and grant them this request, or perhaps He would see other things they couldn't and instruct that no exception was to be made.

What she had to do was trust in His wisdom and goodness, either way. Whatever happened, it was for their best. For all of Israel's best. And for His glory.

Oh, but she wanted to be a part of that. She wanted her sisters to be. She wanted to know that they were walking boldly in His favor, not just slinking along in His shadow, trying to avoid notice.

Other voices had joined in the songs, of course. Hundreds of them. But it was her sisters she heard most clearly, to whom her ears and heart were most attuned. She heard Izik's clear, strong tenor. Uriel's baritone that thrummed pleasantly in her chest. Kap never sang—but he'd found a pipe somewhere and was adding his instrument's voice, its notes piercing the sky with sweet clarity that made her smile around her words.

Her soul still ached with the tragedy of the last two days. She knew from experience that the empty spot left by Abba's death wouldn't heal over—it would just become part of who she was, the wounds that told her story.

But the song reminded her that her story didn't stop here. She simply had to step forward and see what more would be told of it.

CHAPTER FOUR

No'ah might have been known as the sister who never stopped moving, but even she had to admit that the walk from their home on the outskirts of Manasseh's side of camp, abutting the wilderness, to where Moses sat in the judgment seat in the center of Israel felt like the longest journey she had ever made.

It wasn't, of course. She'd crossed to the opposite side of camp countless times. She'd gone with Abba into Shittim or other towns or cities they'd camped near over the years. All of those trips far outdid this one in terms of steps to take or time in which to take them.

But those had all just been to get to a place. To visit a friend. To explore. To trade.

This, though. This was *everything*, and it had energy buzzing through her veins.

Or maybe that was Izik, making literal buzzing noises to mock her, even fluttering his hands at his sides like miniature wings.

He did it with a grin on his face, so she laughed and gave him a shove in the arm. "Careful, Iz, or this bee will sting you."

"Wouldn't be the first time." He acted as though he was about to shove her back, but the squeal of protest from Milcah had him instead simply patting her on the shoulder.

Milcah elbowed her way between them, moving her scowl from one to the other. "If you two break into a game of chase and ruin your clothing and hair, No'ah…"

A few years ago, No'ah would have said, "Then you'll *what*? What will you do?" and would have deliberately run off, at a speed high enough to make her braided hair fall from where it was placed, the flowers and beads fall out of the heavy tresses, and her garment go askew and change its color thanks to the dust she'd kick up.

But she'd finally—mostly—outgrown that instinct. At the very least, she had no desire to ruin her appearance today. Or to irritate her little sister.

Today of all days, they had to look their best. Today of all days, peace needed to prevail between them. Today of all days, she had to curb her perpetual buzzing and try to convince Moses that she was a perfectly respectable young lady, worthy of his favor—and the Lord's.

She pressed her lips against a grin. Maybe, *maybe* she'd be able to pull the wool over Moses's eyes, if he focused more on her sisters than on her. But she knew very well that their all-seeing God knew exactly who she was beneath the lovely drape of her tunic and the jewelry and braids with which Milcah had adorned them all. He should, after all—He'd created her just so. And so, the real trick would be to show Him how she could honor Him just as she was.

Or so she told herself as she slipped back into her place between Iz and Mil and wound her arms around theirs. She couldn't quite refrain from bouncing on her toes as she walked.

Milcah let out a noise that sounded equal parts amused and frustrated. No'ah could understand that—it was how she felt when this particular sister maintained that annoying regal bearing all the time, even when she had no right to be composed and calm. "I can't help it, Mil," she said, knowing the laugh in her voice wouldn't soothe her sister's ruffled feathers any. "We're going to face *Moses*. How could I not be excited?" And nervous. And anxious.

They all were. She knew that. Each of them just showed it in her own way.

Izik reached with the opposite hand to pat the fingers resting on his arm. "The five of you can't help but impress him. What's more, your cause is just. Everyone in Israel has heard of the Shadow and knows what a brave, courageous, God-fearing man he was. Wanting to honor his name is good."

"I know." She'd in fact recited that litany nearly word for word to Mahlah last night as they both lay sleepless upon their beds. And as long as they kept the focus on Abba, they could both breathe in a bit of calm.

As soon as they remembered that *they* were the ones Moses would be seeing, *they* must be judged worthy of Abba's legacy, it all unraveled, and the buzzing took to wing again.

Izik could probably read her mind. That was no doubt why he chuckled and patted her fingers again. "And you're well supported. Take comfort in that too." He nodded to where the elders led them to the center of the congregation and the tabernacle.

Her gaze drifted away from the familiar backs of Simon and the others—to the cloud that hovered over the center of camp.

She'd seen it all her life, anytime she looked east and upward. The visible presence of God. A firm reminder that He was more than an idol, lifeless and crafted by men. He was the God of gods, the Lord of lords, and He was *there*. Right there, always present, always watching over them.

And yet still people forgot Him. Still people turned to the gods who promised pleasure and wealth and indulgence. Still people chose their own ways above His.

Laughter cut into her attention, bringing her gaze back to the people of God rather than the being of God. They *ought* to be a reflection of Him, but they failed at that more often than they succeeded, it seemed. So many events of the last forty years testified to that—the golden calf, the sons of Korah, and most recently, the plague. Though so far as she knew, no new cases had been reported in the last fortnight, since Abba's funeral. Perhaps that meant that everyone who remained in Israel was dedicated fully to God.

She hoped so. Just as she hoped that these two weeks they'd waited to receive an audience with Moses would be enough to have prepared them. The elders had put the time to use, deciding who would represent them, so that Moses knew they had the backing of the whole tribe. They'd recommended that the girls begin their petition with a psalm of praise to God, to showcase not only their talents but their faith in the Lord. Aunts and female cousins had come to advise on what they should wear, to help make new garments, to trade jewelry until they looked perfect.

Well. No'ah sent a smile down the line of her sisters. *They* all looked perfect. *She* would no doubt buzz something out of place before they got to Moses's tent on the east side of the tabernacle, where he would hear their petition. But the fault would be only her own, not through any lack of attention paid by their kinswomen or her sisters.

Mahlah walked a step ahead of the rest of them, her harp in one hand and the fingers of the other twitching through the notes she would play. She'd been practicing the song they'd sing as if she hadn't played it a thousand times before. Hoglah had choreographed a simple dance to accompany the words too. It would be beautiful.

Still, No'ah would have felt more comfortable if the aunts had let her strap her blades to her side. And Mahlah, she knew, would feel unbalanced without her bow and arrows on the shoulder opposite her harp.

The laugh came again, grating on her nerves in a way that made no sense until she followed the sound back to its owner and winced involuntarily. Cozbi. Why did *he* have to come? He was no elder, and he wasn't that close a cousin either. Plus—and she couldn't stress this enough—none of them liked him.

That probably wasn't to her credit. The Law instructed her to love her neighbors, and he was *that*, whether she wanted him to be or not. But he always dismissed her with a single glance—and then started ogling Mahlah and Milcah. Apparently he found their tall, willowy frames attractive, and for that she couldn't fault him. They *were* beautiful, in a way that few other women around them could claim. That didn't mean he should act as he did, though, leering at them all the time, and in a way that made it clear he thought them more a possession to be bought, a trophy to be won, than a helpmeet he could love and respect.

Frankly, she was surprised he even supported this petition. He clearly didn't want a wife with her own ideas, and wouldn't having her own property guarantee she came with a few thoughts on how to use it?

She sucked in a sharp breath that had both Iz and Mil looking over at her, asking, "What?" in unison.

No'ah nodded toward where Cozbi strutted beside his brother and father. "Him. You don't think...you don't think he's coming to *oppose* the petition, do you?"

Izik frowned. "Why would he do that?"

Milcah snorted, clearly following No'ah's thoughts without trouble. "Because giving women an inheritance would imply we have worth, value—it would put us on a footing with men more equal than he would like. He has to contradict everything a woman says, you know. Even if we observe the day is lovely, he feels the need to point out that there's a cloud on the horizon or the temperature is just a bit too something."

Izik snorted now too, and it sounded amused. "He's a real oaf, without question. But I don't think he'll oppose it."

"You don't?" No'ah wanted to cling to that hope—because she was none too sure what Moses would do if anyone spoke out against them. But how could Izik be so sure?

He sent her a crooked smile. "Think about it, No. He has his sights set on Mahlah. What would make her even more desirable, do you think? Perhaps...an inheritance? It would double his holdings, then. If she gets the firstborn son's portion, then combined with his own second-son's portion, he'd own more than his brother, despite being the younger."

No'ah's lips fell open a long moment before she could wrap her tongue around any words. "But…" Apparently that was the only word she could find even after that moment, and it hardly did justice to the sudden torrent of thoughts lashing down in her mind.

Izik sent her a steady, steadying look. "I know. I know this whole plea is about getting your father's portion for *you*. All of you. But think about it realistically, No'ah. When each of you marries, you won't just maintain that land independently and pass it along to daughters. You'll be joining it with your husbands' land, and it'll then go to *your* sons."

Of course that made sense. But somehow she hadn't thought of it before. In all their dreaming and wondering and fearing, the practical side of what a potential inheritance actually looked like hadn't once entered their conversations, because…well, because marriages still seemed so unreal to them. Even with Uriel finding excuses to visit nearly every day, No'ah hadn't wrapped her mind or heart around any of her sisters actually leaving Abba's household. To her, thoughts of his inheritance meant a means of staying together, if they chose. Of having a place, someday, together.

But that was foolish. She knew that. None of them *really* wanted to stay home forever. They wanted their *own* homes. Husbands. Children. They wanted to put down roots in the Promised Land someday soon. To grow their own food and feast on it. To build houses of stone and brick. To bake in ovens, not just over a campfire, as they'd seen people in the cities doing.

How could a thing shine like the stars in the heavens and yet feel every bit as far away too? Yet be so close?

She'd been looking Cozbi's way too long. He glanced over, caught her staring narrowed-eyed at him, and sent her the same sneer he always sent her. Then his gaze drifted a fraction, toward Milcah. Then Mahlah.

Snake. Well, he could try all he wanted to slither into their inheritance—assuming they got one—but it would be to no avail. None of her sisters were senseless enough to give him a second glance.

Izik cleared his throat. "Little Bee, you may want to wipe that scowl off your face and remember your purpose." He nodded ahead of them, where the cloud hovered over the tabernacle.

While her thoughts hummed and buzzed, her feet had bounced her closer and closer to their destination. They were nearly through the Levitical Sons of Gersham, who camped between the three western tribes and the tabernacle. The gorgeous tapestry walls were in view now, and No'ah's pulse kicked up more with each thread her eyes traced.

Purple, scarlet, sapphire. Gold and silver. It all flashed and danced across the thick fabric, telling a story with its beauty of God's majesty, of the One who created the world and all that was in it.

Imma had helped embroider a section, as most of the women had nearly forty years ago. Imma had been a girl at the time, only ten when Moses descended from Mount Sinai with the Commandments and the instruction for the tabernacle's construction. But she was a girl who had been born into captivity in Egypt, which meant a girl who knew how to work. Under the tutelage of *her* imma, she'd already been a master with needle and thread. She'd been graced with the honor of wielding it for the Lord, and she'd told the story to her daughters in turn.

Well. She'd told it to the four of them she'd gotten to know, though only No'ah and Mahlah remembered any of her tales. They'd had to be the ones to tell them to Hoglah and Milcah, and especially to Tirzah.

She hoped they'd honored her, kept her memory alive enough for the younger ones. She hoped that, wherever their souls had gone when they fled their bodies, Abba and Imma were together again.

She hoped she and her sisters made them proud today.

Simon and the other elders led them through the camp of Levi that encircled the tabernacle, from the Gershonites through the sons of Kohath, and then finally into the western side of Levi, where Moses and Eleazar and the other priests set up their tents.

No'ah had to fight the urge to run a circle around her sisters, to give this sizzle of energy inside her somewhere to go. And then, to make matters worse, Izik stepped away, sending her an encouraging smile, a teasing wink, and a shooing motion. He joined Kap and Uriel, who had also just peeled off from Mahlah's side and were aimed toward their father, who strode nearer to Simon than the girls.

No'ah sucked in a long breath and exchanged a wide-eyed glance with Milcah, Hoglah, and Tirzah. They then all sent bolstering smiles to Mahlah, who cast a panic-stricken look at them over her shoulder.

Poor Mahl. She looked as though she might lose her breakfast. Or faint. Or just run crying back to the tents of Manasseh. No'ah knew very well that the only thing holding her sister to her place in the procession was the weight of responsibility for the rest of them.

No'ah glanced at her younger sisters again. The plan had been to enter Moses's tent this way, clearly demonstrating that Mahlah, as the eldest sister, would be appealing for the role of firstborn son, with the rest of them as later-born ones.

But they *weren't* sons. They were daughters. Sisters. And though Mahlah had stepped into Imma's shoes and raised them, they'd each learned how best to support each other. She *wasn't* their mother, she was their sister. Which meant she wasn't alone before them with Abba gone. They were together.

No'ah leaned forward to catch the gazes of the other three, then glanced toward Mahlah, quaking in her sandals. No words were needed for instruction—when she let go of Milcah's arm and caught up her fingers, tugging, the others caught on immediately and broke into twos. She and Milcah moved to Mahlah's right side, Hoglah and Tirzah to her left. They joined arms, creating a clear statement.

Together. Sisters.

Mahlah looked down at her and smiled. "This wasn't the plan."

No'ah grinned back. "New plan. Better plan."

Mahlah laughed, and more importantly, relaxed a little. "Much better plan."

Levites milled around them, offering only vague smiles of greeting that gave no indicator of the mood of their leader today. Not that Moses's judgments were known to rely on his mood—after all, the Most High wasn't prey to human moodiness, and it was to Him that Moses listened. Even so, No'ah could feel the tension coursing through the line of the five of them, and it didn't ease as they followed the tribal elders into a large tent.

Moses sat at the front. He was an old man, she knew—older than anyone else left in Israel. But he didn't *look* it. He still looked energetic and vibrant, his skin taut, his hair still plenty dark amidst the silver. And he smiled at them. *That* eased a bit of her tension.

Here was the man who'd been raised in Pharaoh's palace. Who had fled to Midian when he killed an Egyptian who had beaten a Hebrew. Who had returned from the desert to lead God's people to freedom. Here was the man who had parted the Red Sea. Who had climbed the Mount to receive the very finger-written Words of God. Who had seen Him, if only from behind. Here was the man who heard His voice and knew His name.

Smiling at *them.*

No'ah didn't know whether to smile back or bow her head in respect. She opted for the dip of her chin, since that's what Mahlah did, and the line of elders who stood before them.

Simon was speaking—was already halfway through his practiced speech, which meant that No'ah hadn't been paying as much attention to him as she should have been. Too busy chasing the flitting of her thoughts over all Moses had been and done and seen. But she forced her focus upon the words, now, listening and watching the leader as *he* listened.

He didn't look particularly outraged by the request…but surprised, yes. That was clear by the way he sat up straighter when Simon said, "his daughters in his stead" and blinked at them. The smile hadn't totally fallen from his lips, but it had frozen. His gaze swept down the line of sisters as Simon finished his petition on behalf of the elders of Manasseh.

Moses let silence fall for one beat of her heart. Two. "Zelophehad—the same Zelophehad renowned for his scouting and defense of the camp? Who tried to fight in battles when he was but a boy? Called the Shadow?"

Simon bowed at the waist. "The same, my lord. He was a man beloved by all, respected by all, and who loved the Lord with all his heart."

"So then not a victim of the plague? Nor one of the sons of Korah struck down?"

"No!" Simon jerked upright, the fury in his voice matching the burning of it in her own chest. "He was a victim of violence—struck in the back by a Moabite dagger while he was praying outside camp two weeks ago."

"Hmm. And these are his five daughters? Let me see them." He motioned with his hand, and Simon and the other elders cleared out of the way, breaking into two groups and moving to either side of them.

It was their cue to begin their presentation…which was supposed to begin with Mahlah stepping forward and speaking the lines they'd composed together, had practiced together scores of times.

Only Mahlah just stood there, panic in her eyes again.

Well. Good thing she had sisters. No'ah pinched the inside of her arm and, when she jerked, nudged her forward.

Mahlah would scold her for it later. But for now, she simply jumped into action, curtsying low and saying, "If it pleases you, my lord, we would like to share our father's favorite hymn with you."

He could refuse, of course—say he hadn't time for a performance, that there were a hundred other petitions he had to hear yet today. They were prepared for that, prepared to simply introduce themselves and then state their plea.

But Moses renewed his smile, moving it from Mahlah to the rest of them in turn. He leaned back in his chair. "Of course. I would love to hear the Shadow's favorite song."

Mahlah's small harp had been slung over her shoulder—she pulled it forward now, and though No'ah couldn't see her face, she knew what it would look like. Mahlah would close her eyes. That peace that came only with music would turn her always-lovely face into a work of unparalleled beauty, and then she titled her head just so, as if letting the music drift into her ear from heaven. And she strummed.

They all picked up their lines, voices blending together in practiced harmony as they sang of the greatness of I Am. As they sang, the four of them moved in the simple, elegant dance Hoglah had come up with—movements slow and graceful and fluid.

Mahlah swayed along with them, moving a foot out now and then and back in to mimic their movements behind her, but that was all she attempted while holding the harp. They'd tried to convince her to dance fully with them, but that had proven a disaster that kept them laughing for an hour.

The song could go on forever if the singer wanted, looping and repeating over and again. None of their nerves could handle that though, so they'd agreed to keep it short. They hit their final note, Mahlah added a flourish on the harp, and their arms, which had ended raised in praise, all lowered together.

Only then did No'ah dare to glance once more at Moses.

He was smiling.

CHAPTER FIVE

Mahlah felt as out of breath as if she'd been dancing with her sisters, though she'd barely even raised her voice in the song, knowing they'd carry it well enough without her. It took her a long moment to convince herself to open her eyes and see what their leader had thought of their performance.

No, not *performance*. It hadn't been about that. It had been…a demonstration. Of what Abba had taught them. Who he'd raised them to be. The love of God he'd instilled in them all.

She wanted to spin around to exchange smiles with her sisters, but instead she simply moved the harp around again and finally dragged her gaze back to where Moses sat in his seat.

He was smiling. Breath too long pent-up inside her gushed out, and Mahlah dipped her head once more in respect before clearing the anxiety from her throat and making herself smile back.

Perhaps it started out forced—but it didn't stay that way. Not when she considered her sisters and how Moses must see them. Four young women, possessed of all the attributes young women should be. Beautiful and demure, talented and faithful, loving and loyal.

"Thank you for welcoming us, my lord," she said, grateful that her voice sounded sure and strong. "And for allowing us to show you a bit of our father's legacy—one of faith and love for the Lord. When our elders suggested we come and make this petition to you, we agreed not out of any selfishness on our own parts but out of the deepest love and respect for our father."

She made herself meet his gaze and found it warm. Thoughtful. Her fingers still clutched the strap of her harp. "Everyone in Israel knows our father as a man of integrity and of the deepest heart. It was his uncompromising love for our mother that left him without a male heir. After she died giving birth to my youngest sister, Tirzah, he never had the heart to remarry. Though few understood it, we knew that it was because he valued her memory above an heir, and he always assured us he loved us, his daughters, as much as he could any son."

Would that be to his credit in Moses's eyes, or a mark against him? She didn't know, couldn't know. But for her part, it didn't matter. She would say the truth, only the truth, and let God and Moses decide what it meant.

"He was a man of bravery, of strength, of boldness, but also a man of compassion, of good humor, and of gentleness with his family. He pursued the Lord with his whole heart and cared for his family from the outpouring of that devotion. And that, my lord, is why he deserves to be remembered among his brothers when we take the Promised Land."

She straightened her spine, lifted her chin. For Abba. For Abba, she would stand as tall as any other man here, taller than quite a few. For Abba, she wouldn't let her spine bend or her head dip, as it so often did when she just wanted to blend in with the other girls. For Abba, she would show what he'd passed down to her. "Zelophehad had no sons—but he has five daughters. We ask, my lord, that you grant us our father's portion among the tribe of Manasseh, so that his name may live on in the generations to come."

Moses said nothing at first, just tapped a fingertip to his lips. He was looking at her, yes, but not *just* at her, or so it seemed. She imagined he was looking at the whole situation. At all it represented. At the impact his judgment would have, not only on them but on generations to come, rippling out well beyond their one tribe.

His gaze shifted, moving just as thoughtfully over her sisters, then darting momentarily to the elders before landing once more on Mahlah. He shifted, sat up straighter. "This is a matter of the gravest importance—a decision that isn't just for your family, young lady, but for *all* of Israel, from this moment but moving forward as we do. I must take the question directly to the Lord." He stood, and the whole congregation within the tent shifted. He stayed them with a raised hand. "Please, wait here for a while. Relax. I will either be back soon or will let Joshua know that you ought to return to your homes. If that happens, I will call for you all to reconvene when I have an answer."

Mahlah held her place until Moses disappeared behind a curtain, and then she sagged, sucked in a long breath, and spun to face her sisters. They surged around her, four different streams of encouragement flooding her ears. She just smiled and did her best to hold them all tight. "Did I forget anything? Say anything wrong?"

No'ah vibrated beside her. "I have no idea. It all sounded perfect to me. You did great, Mahl."

"I couldn't have said it better," Milcah said.

Hoglah nodded. "You were eloquence and grace."

"I know we would have made Abba proud." Tirzah gave them another squeeze.

Mahlah sniffled a bit at that but then forced the tears away and renewed her smile. There had been enough tears every other day, and there would be plenty more in the future, whenever she considered their loss or remembered the horror of Abba with that dagger in his back. But for now, today, here in this time of unknowing, she would simply hope. Simply be glad that they had reflected well on their father and their family.

Eventually, they loosened their knot and let Simon guide them toward mats they could sit on while they waited. Easy chatter sprang up—the kind that could be tossed aside just as readily if and when Moses returned. Mahlah let it wash over her, absently fixed a spray of flowers threatening to escape No'ah's hair, and found her gaze wandering through the tent. Who all had come in with them? Had Uriel?

She didn't see him in here, nor even Kapriel or Izik, though Seth was just ducking back inside. The others must be waiting outside—in which case, he'd probably ducked out to tell them how it was going thus far.

Her heart thumped at the thought of Uriel standing right outside. He'd be talking to Kap and Iz, laughing with them, perhaps, wondering what Moses would say. Wondering if it would impact his own future.

Mahlah pulled her harp into her lap, in part to keep it from digging into her back…in part because her fingers craved the soothing strings. She strummed them softly, one melody chasing another without settling entirely. Abiram stood there beside Simon, smiling and looking at ease. He'd told her just that morning that he would honor Abba's wishes. That they could each choose their own husbands…as long as they weighed his and their other uncles' advice and didn't rush into anything.

No'ah had admitted that she'd asked him about it soon after Abba's death, and that he'd told her the same then—but then had come the petition and the waiting and the planning, and a thousand other details to take care of, so such thoughts had been pushed aside. Understandably. It wasn't as though any of them would be making any decisions about husbands until their mourning period was over, at the least.

But her uncles would honor Abba's desires. They would let them have a voice in their matches—the loudest voices. They would let them follow their hearts. No matter what Moses determined, it meant that the future was *theirs.* Theirs not just to participate in but to help direct. It meant that she could get to know Uriel without wondering if an uncle would just arrange another betrothal for her without her knowing it.

She didn't have to fear falling in love with one man and being forced to marry someone else instead. A fear she hadn't even realized had sunk its teeth into her, alleviated.

"You know," No'ah whispered, quietly enough that no one else would be able to hear over the harp and the general chatter, "you're going to have everyone wondering which of the young men out there you're pining for, if you keep looking toward the door like that."

Mahlah's finger slipped off the string it had been about to pluck, and it took her a beat to pick up her place again. Fire scorched her cheeks. "I don't know what you're talking about."

Light glimmered in her sister's eyes—a light that had been dimmed too much by recent events. It was good to see it sparkling again now, even if it was at her expense. "I've been waiting and waiting for you to tell me, you know. Any other situation, I would have lost patience long ago."

Mahlah tried glancing away, weighing the likelihood of No'ah believing her if she played dumb. But given that her glance went right back to the tent's door flap and the young men she knew were outside it, *that* was probably useless. She sighed.

No'ah chuckled. "You know you can trust me with this. I won't breathe a word. Has Uriel said anything to you yet? About his intentions?"

Well then. She'd not only discovered that Mahlah's heart had begun leaning in a certain direction, she'd even deduced who had inspired it. No point then in claiming ignorance. Mahlah bit her lip and gave one short nod of her head. "The morning...*that* morning. Before."

"Oh." In a flash, the teasing gleam was muted by the recognition, the grief, the pain. And the knot in her brow said she also understood the strange tangle of guilt and hope and fear that had taken up residence in Mahlah's chest. "What horrible timing. Or perhaps...perhaps perfect timing. A sliver of light in a time so very dark."

She understood it even better than Mahlah had. She alternated between appreciating that twinkle of light and feeling as though she was betraying Abba by clinging to it. Wouldn't a proper daughter have been carried away by the darkness? Or finding hope in her sisters' smiles instead of a man's? Shouldn't she have wanted to carry on for *them*, not for herself?

No'ah poked a finger into Mahlah's arm. "You're doing it again."

Mahlah shrugged the offending digit away. "Doing what?"

"Trying to convince yourself that your own happiness doesn't matter. Won't you stop that? We all *want* you to be happy, to find a man you love enough to marry. We want to dance at your wedding and be aunts and be able to ask you for advice on marital things when it's our turn."

Mahlah smiled, then grinned, then felt a new flush in her cheeks at her sister's list. Of course, it all faded into another frown. "Are you saying that I'm failing you all by *not* being married already, so that I can—"

"Mahlah!" Laughing, No'ah halted her with a hand over her mouth, as she'd been doing since they were children—and which Mahlah had *thought* she'd broken her of a decade ago. "Hush. You haven't failed anyone or at anything in your entire life. Ever. Stop pretending it's actually a valid fear and listen to what I'm *saying*." Dropping her fingers, she leaned close. "Be happy. We want you to be. We *need* you to be."

"Be happy," Mahlah echoed, fingers dancing over the strings. She drew in a long breath. "I…I want to be. I do." Her lips curled up into a smile. "I really do. And I think…I think he may…"

"Moses returns!"

That hadn't taken long—did that mean good news or bad? Mahlah let No'ah haul her to her feet, let Tirzah take her harp and Milcah fuss with her clothes and Hoglah tuck something into her hair that must have come loose. They scurried back into their places before the judgment seat, the elders once again flanking them, but this time standing in their line rather than off to the sides.

Abiram leaned forward, caught her gaze, and sent her an encouraging smile. In his eyes she could read the same words he'd spoken to her that morning when he came to fetch them. *Whatever happens, the Lord will be glorified through it, and it will be for your best good.*

She'd nodded then because she'd needed the words. She nodded now because she knew they were true. *Our best good.*

Someone held back the curtain behind which Moses had vanished, and he reemerged, his face set in a pleasant expression that could either mean good news or simply that he was at peace with what the Lord had told him. How was she to know?

He still moved with the energy of a man in his prime, no shuffling in his steps as he angled toward the chair, no hunch in his back as he sat. Mahlah had watched a generation die before her eyes—the ones who had doubted the word of Caleb and Joshua and listened instead to the faithless spies of Canaan forty years ago. She'd watched her grandparents and her parents' aunts and uncles shrivel and weaken when they weren't— so they'd said—old enough to warrant it. They'd claimed that they aged too fast those forty years, that though their clothes and shoes never wore out, it seemed their flesh did all the faster.

Yet there was Moses, who looked so young still. Because he'd seen God? Because he heard Him? Had the same encounters that had made his face glow—so much that he'd needed to veil it—lit a fire of life within him too?

Musings that at least served to occupy her while the leader took his seat, even if she had no answers.

Moses didn't look to be in any great rush, but neither did he take too much time getting comfortable. He simply sat, took a moment to clear his throat, and then looked out at them. At *her*, then her sisters, and only then to the elders of the tribe.

Again he smiled. "I have taken the question before the Lord, and He has answered. It is good and fair that the daughters of Zelophehad inherit their father's portion in the Land when the Children of Israel take it. It is fitting that he be remembered and that he have a legacy among his brethren. And so it shall be for any man in Israel, now or after the Land is ours, who dies without a son but has daughters. They shall inherit as sons would, so that their father's name is not snuffed out. If he has no daughters, his brothers shall inherit his portion. And if he has no brothers, then his nearest relative."

Mahlah could only stare at him as the words sank in, as her sisters grabbed her fingers and squeezed, as happy words of thanksgiving and praise to God sprang from the lips of the elders. She heard them all, felt them all, but it still it seemed as though she were in a bubble, apart from it all.

Until Moses looked at her again. He held her gaze, and she got the feeling he saw all her hopes and dreams and fears, how desperately she wanted to honor her father, how worried she was that she'd fail him. Moses had probably wrestled with everything she could possibly feel and a million other things besides over the years. But he smiled, and it was like a gift of peace and confidence. He nodded, and had she not still been staring at him, she never would have been able to read the words on his lips that she couldn't hear over the chatter.

"The Lord is pleased with you."

For a moment she doubted that she had read his lips correctly. But his smile was the sort of proud, warm smile that Abba had always worn when they sang for him—or hit the target he'd set up with whatever weapon he'd put in their hands that day. The kind that said he was pleased not because of what they did or how they did it, but because they'd *wanted* to please him.

Warmth spread through her chest, and tears—far different from the ones she'd been crying lately—stung her eyes.

Their God was a fearsome God. A God of fire and cloud, a God of creation and destruction, a God who purged impurity and handed down Law.

But their God, unlike any other god in all the lands, was more than that too—He was a God of love. A God who called them His children. Who parted the sea for them and who instructed them so that they could become a people worthy of being called His own. He was a God who was not distant, thundering in the heavens and rumbling in the mountains, but who was *here*. Who ordered the world but also cared about five orphaned daughters, and the father who deserved to be remembered.

She splayed a hand over the beautiful ache in her chest, blinked against the crystal tears that didn't so much as budge, and inclined her head toward Moses. There were no words to thank him for this.

Chaos danced her out of the tent with her sisters, chaos in the form of laughter and shouts and the joy of her tribal elders, her uncles and cousins. Abiram caught them each in a hug, his face brighter than it had been since Keturah safely delivered him twin boys six years ago.

She searched the crowd outside for Uriel, but she couldn't spot anyone in particular, given that Abiram gave her a happy shake, and then No'ah spun her around, and then Simon was there, clapping a fatherly hand to her shoulder and saying something about how everything would change for them now.

Her head still spun even after No'ah had let her go. Laughter crowded her throat as she raised a hand to rest against her ear, willing the world to steady. "I know," she said to Simon. Most of it wouldn't come up for a while yet, until after they actually entered the Promised Land. But even so, there were changes. Plenty of them. Too many. Even though the uncles had granted that they were capable of remaining in Abba's tent without any guardians present, being all of age, there had been a hundred smaller things that had shifted.

But this one, at least, was good. What was theirs would stay theirs. What would have been Abba's would be theirs.

"Congratulations, Mahlah."

The voice doused some of the joy—partly because it was Cozbi's and partly because it wasn't Uriel's. Still, she wouldn't let it ebb entirely, even if she was careful to keep her smile neutral as she turned it toward Cozbi. "Thank you. I was nervous."

"Nonsense. How could Moses have refused you?"

She had to clench her teeth and take a deep breath. "Just because it seemed good and fair to us didn't mean the Lord would see it that way, given that He knows so much more than we do. Moses rules as the Lord—"

"He doesn't take *every* decision directly to God, though. He could have easily made a ruling then and there, and he would have ruled in your favor."

But he hadn't, and who was to say what he would have done if he had? All that mattered was what *had* happened. Not that she meant to start an argument over hypotheticals. Knowing her smile was tight and not exactly regretting that, she said, "Regardless, I am both grateful and glad to have it finished."

"Indeed." He stood a little taller, though he was still a bit shorter than she was. "I wanted to let you know that I've spoken to my father, who intends to speak to your uncles. I expect something can be arranged quickly. We could announce a betrothal as soon as your mourning is complete."

Was it fury that flashed over her, hot and then cold? Frustration? Disgust? She didn't know the proper word, but it stole her words away and left her clenching her teeth again, curling her hands into fists too.

Where was her harp? Did one of her sisters still have it? It hadn't been left in Moses's tent, had it? Not that it would have provided any protection from Cozbi's plans for her life, but it would have been comfort, anyway.

"Actually, my young friend…" Abiram, bless him, slipped up beside her, a fatherly arm around her shoulders but his gaze focused on Cozbi. He had a mild smile on his lips. "We'll be honoring the Shadow's wishes for his daughters. We'll not just be arranging their betrothals. They'll choose their own husbands and, assuming we approve their selections, *then* I'll begin betrothal negotiations."

Cozbi's face went still. Tight. Hard. His expression didn't exactly change, it just…solidified. It made his blink look ominous. "You can't be serious. It isn't how it's done. Letting all five of them choose? You could be saddled with them for years!"

Saddled with them? Mahlah's fingernails dug into her palms.

Abiram gave her shoulder a squeeze and chuckled. "Oh, I doubt that. I daresay every unmarried young man in Israel will be clamoring to get to know them now. They'll have no shortage of options."

Wait. "What? Why—?"

Abiram sent her an amused look. "You and your sisters are now the only female inheritors in the entire nation. Anyone who marries you will in effect have a double portion of the Promised Land. You think that won't bring everyone to meet you?"

Was that what Simon had meant by things changing?

Of course it was. Because of *course* it would. And she was a complete fool for not considering that, for not realizing that it could quickly become a problem. How were they to know who really liked *them* and who was only after what was theirs?

"Mahlah!" Kapriel's voice this time, and Uriel was only a step behind him. Kap caught her about the waist, spun her around once to make her laugh, and then put her down—whether by design or accident—so that she landed right in front of Uriel, who steadied her with a hand to her back and a warm, secret smile.

It took no effort at all to return it. And peace settled over the uncertainty. He'd liked her before Abba died. Before there was any thought of inheritances. Uriel, at least, she could be sure of.

And now, with her uncles' blessings, she could see what exactly that meant.

CHAPTER SIX

They were swarming like ants on a hill—and No'ah hated ants. For that matter, she wasn't fond of *any* insect swarm, even the bees that she wanted to feel an affinity with, given Izik's nickname for her. But there was the truth: one bee was friendly and fun. A whole swarm of them not only made her skin crawl, they were dangerous.

And that was the impression she got from *this* swarm too. Dangerous.

She sidestepped yet another Israelite man oh-so-eager to win the attention of one of her sisters and stepped on another's foot in the process. "Sorry!" The word came out by reflex, but she wasn't entirely sure she meant it, given the anger that flashed over that fellow's face.

Anyone who would get angry over one of the Five Daughters—as they were apparently being called—accidentally stepping on his foot got immediately crossed off her list. Especially when it was just petite little *her*, not towering Mahlah. It wasn't as if she possibly could have hurt him.

"Be more careful, girl," the man spat at her. "And refill my cup."

She looked from his outstretched cup to the waterskin in her hands—the one she'd just filled at the river for her sisters'

needs for the evening. "I beg your pardon?" Under normal cir-
cumstances, she'd be happy to serve any guests to their tent.

But these people weren't guests. They were land-seeking,
selfish oafs only out to win a double portion, who had arrived
uninvited and swarmed until one uncle or another dismissed
them every evening. There were so many that it was impossible
to host them inside—they instead swarmed out over the landscape like insects, covering every rock and tree stump in sight.
Or so it seemed.

The man changed tactics, putting on a smile. "Forgive
me—I'm short-tempered after waiting hours for an introduction I may never get. Could I trouble you for a drink? It's hot
out here."

That nearly sounded human. Too bad for him that she'd
already seen a glimpse of his inner insect. Even so, No'ah lifted
the waterskin, tilting the spout so it filled his cup halfway.
But only halfway. "Forgive me," she said, imitating his too-sweet
tone. "There are many people here, and all of them are hot
and will no doubt be demanding I solve that for them."

The man at least had the grace to offer a sheepish smile.
"Quite a gathering, isn't it? I'm beginning to despair of ever
meeting your...cousins?"

Ah, so that was his new strategy. He'd apparently decided
that anyone serving—obviously what he'd assumed she was
doing—would be a fairly close relative to the Five Daughters,
to have either volunteered for or been drafted into the duty.

Perhaps she took a bit too much delight in offering him
her best, mocking imitation of Milcah's regal smile and lifting

her chin. "Sisters. But don't worry. I'll tell the others *all* about your gracious greeting to the Second Daughter."

Her new name, it seemed. She might have grumbled more about it, if Mahlah didn't have it so much worse, being the First. *She* was the one everyone really wanted to win over, given that she would receive the firstborn son's double portion. And with no parent or sisters to care for with that extra amount, given that they had their own, that simply meant extra wealth. An extra portion of their herds. Extra land, and all it provided. Extra grain once they grew it, extra wine, extra *everything*.

Izik, amusement in his eyes, had asked her if she was jealous. She hadn't stopped laughing for minutes. Poor Mahlah— she'd trade that extra for a bit of peace in a heartbeat, No'ah knew. She'd have to be a madwoman to want to take it on instead of her capable sister.

The stranger's face went panicked, apologies tripping off his tongue now, but No'ah didn't stick around to hear them. Yes, he was hot and tired and no doubt frustrated with himself for wasting a big portion of his day on what turned out to be a useless endeavor. But that didn't give him any right to be rude and demanding. And what if it had been sweet-natured Hoglah he'd treated so, or young Tirzah?

"Why do I feel like I ought to don some armor to get within ten feet of you?"

She looked up at Izik's voice and found him easily enough. He was weaving his way through the gathering of men with the sort of easy stealth he'd learned from years of chasing after— and hiding from—Kapriel and his friends. No'ah grinned. "At

---

least water is my only weapon just now." She hefted the filled bag in proof.

He took it from her without asking if she wanted or needed him to, as he always did. She didn't mind carrying it. She didn't mind letting *him* do it either. His eyes skimmed over the dozens—hundreds—thousands?—of marrying-age men. "Is it my imagination, or are there even more today than yesterday?"

"I have no idea. I've given up counting. Though at least it's only in the evenings now, since your father forbade anyone from interrupting the day's work." Even looking out at the group generally meant a few seemed to think she was looking at *them*—and apparently unlike the fellow a minute ago, these knew who she was. Their faces lit, and it looked as though they were about to charge over their companions, vault over rocks, sprout wings, and fly to get to her.

In self-defense, she slid her arm through Izik's and smiled up at him. "I'm about to tell Abiram to arrange something for me, just to save myself from actually having to meet all these people in search of some…some emotion I'm not sure I'll ever feel anyway."

Izik, obviously knowing what she was about—given that they'd performed the ruse no fewer than five times in the last five days—leaned close and guided her back toward her tent, doing a decent job of looking smitten. Good enough that she wondered who he'd been studying to pull it off. Uriel, perhaps? He'd been doting on Mahlah in a way that might have made her roll her eyes had it been anyone but Mahlah. "You think Abiram could wade through everyone here any quicker than you can? He'd be so determined to find the absolute best match that he'd be at it for years, examining everyone's lineage and personality and traits and habits and whether this one chews his fingernails or that one chews with his mouth open or—"

She laughed, her bad mood flitting away as she did. "Can't you come earlier in the day, Iz? Before the crowds show up?"

"If you can convince Abba he doesn't need me, I'll be here." Spotting something that made him scowl, he steered her between her tent and their closest neighbor's instead of inside.

She glanced around, trying to spot what he had. "What is it?"

"Cozbi—with Danijel." He'd dropped his voice to a whisper, and it only took her a moment to understand why. Rolling onto his toes, he crept closer to the side of Danijel's tent—the one right beside theirs. Danijel's father and her own had been first cousins, which made him one of her closer relatives…and he'd been none too happy when his own proposal for Mahlah's hand had been met with the same now-practiced deferral from Abiram.

If he and Cozbi were stealing inside for a private conversation, it couldn't be anything good. Well, she supposed it *could*, to be fair. They were cousins too, after all, though more distant. There could be any number of things they'd want to talk about that were none of her business, and if she heard talk of horses or donkeys or sheep or cattle coming through the thick tent walls, she'd tug Izik right back to her own door.

"Well, what are we supposed to do?" Danijel was asking, frustration in his tone. "It looks as if every unmarried man in all of Israel is outside!"

"I know. I imagine some of them will lose interest soon enough, when they realize the sisters don't intend to meet each and every one of them." Cozbi didn't actually sound convinced of that.

Danijel snorted. "Or else Abiram's suggestion will prevail, and they *will* meet each one for a few minutes. Like royalty holding court, with everyone ushered in for a brief petition before being tossed out again."

No'ah wrinkled her nose at the very thought. Abiram *had* been trying to convince them to do that, to bring some order to the chaos. No one had any interest in it, of course. Mahlah already knew whose attention she wanted, No'ah was convinced she wouldn't learn anything useful about anyone in an official introduction, and the younger girls had declared it all so overwhelming that they hid away in their partition rather than meeting *anyone*, more often than not.

"One thing in our favor—those girls are all so independent and stubborn, they'll probably send the masses away soon enough." Cozbi snorted. "Then those of us who actually know them will have a better chance of convincing them."

Danijel granted the point with a sigh. "Perhaps. I suppose we'll see, won't we? But I, for one, won't be here watching it all much. The heifers in calf could go into labor any day now."

No'ah tugged Izik away from Danijel's walls, though rather than duck into her own, she kept going, deeper into camp. It ought to be fairly empty of unmarried men, anyway, given that they were all back there.

Izik patted the waterskin. "Are your sisters waiting for this?"

She shrugged. "I sent myself out for it just to get away. Our pots aren't actually empty yet. Or weren't when I left. Though I suppose if all the *guests* have demanded drinks…"

Izik chuckled and tilted his head back to watch a bird soar overhead. "Cozbi and Danijel aren't wrong that the ranks will thin out on their own soon as people get discouraged and give it up."

May the Lord hasten the day. "But?" She could hear that he'd left something unsaid, though she wasn't sure what it was.

He looked over at her, the golden evening sun catching on the amber flecks in his otherwise dark brown eyes. "But…that will still leave plenty. And unfortunately, some of the most determined will be the most deceptive. Like Cozbi. The ones who will do or say anything to get what they want."

She thought of the demanding fellow whose foot she'd stepped on. Chances were good that he was a nice enough man, just caught in a bad moment. But even so, he served as a reminder that everyone had hidden depths that only flashed out under the right provocation. And in a short time frame, such as trying to convince a girl to marry you and her guardian that you were perfectly upright, anyone could lie. She pursed her lips. "You're right. Do you have a solution to this problem or merely an observation?"

Izik grinned, that mischievous flash of teeth that had convinced her as a toddler to follow wherever he led—or tug him along wherever she wanted to go. "When do I not have a plan?"

Laughter warmed her belly and spilled from her lips. "Allow me to rephrase: What do you suggest we do?"

He straightened, lifted his chin, and did his best comical imitation of Kapriel. "Follow the example set forth by Joshua of Nun, of course."

When did Moses's second in command ever have to deal with—"Oh! You mean spy on people?"

As if he actually had to convince her of the wisdom, he leaned a little closer, hands gesturing widely. "Think about it. No one is going to show their true colors to you all when at your tent. They will all be on their best behavior, trying to win not only attention but esteem. But when they *leave*—that's when they'll be complaining or scheming with their friends and family. So all we have to do is what we just did. Follow them back to their own tents and listen."

If Mahlah heard this plan, she'd get that crease between her brows that said she disapproved, even if she hadn't sorted out the words yet to say why. She'd start sputtering about how it wasn't proper or wasn't kind or didn't give people the benefit of the doubt, how a young lady shouldn't do such things or how badly it would reflect on the family if she were caught, or how, if she really did find someone with dark secrets, they could grow violent if they discovered her.

All reasonable arguments, really.

None of them did a thing to keep the grin from taking over No'ah's mouth. "I like it. By 'we,' you do mean both of us doing this spying, right? Because I don't want to do it alone, but I'm not about to let you have all the fun without me."

Izik chuckled. "Of course I mean the two of us. And I already have a plan. We won't be part of the actual evening gatherings, Kap and I—but I'll be waiting for the last of the fellows to leave and will note where they live. You pay attention to who seems to be catching your sisters' eyes or looks the most promising. Slip over to our usual meeting spot when they leave, and we'll follow them. Listen for a while."

Simple and effective. She nodded. "Perfect." Although she couldn't resist a tease. "But why won't you and Kap be there? Shouldn't you be trying to win over Tirzah or Hoglah? And you know Milcah's always been fond of Kap."

It had been the favorite joke when they were younger, the way tiny Milcah had followed Kapriel around, always wanting him to play with her or carry her. It had been a point of exasperation for the ten-year-old, but he'd been kind. Mostly.

Izik grimaced. "Your sisters are great...as sisters. I want to make sure they don't marry someone with a hidden cruel streak, but that someone won't be me. And Kap has this idea of not marrying until after we take the Promised Land, so that he can fight any battles we need to fight without fearing he's leaving a widow behind."

Her feet came to a halt at that, wide eyes focused on Izik's face. Everyone knew they'd be advancing soon, that the places the Lord chose for their camps were leading them closer to the Promised Land, back to the place where the spies and the people had failed forty years before. The last of the old generation had died not four months ago—the plague had cleared out any unfaithful men from the younger generation. They knew that soon the time would come to advance. She knew her generation of men were eager to prove themselves, eager to follow the Lord into what He'd promised them.

She just hadn't paused to think that it could mean death for individuals, even if God had promised victory to the people. She hadn't really stopped to consider that battles would be fought at all, despite having watched Kap and Izik and Uriel and countless others train with swords and spears outside camp for the last several years. It had been entertainment for her and the other young women, nothing more. A chance to admire their forms and graceful movements. Not actual *war* preparation.

She'd thought of it, rather, as she had Abba's training of *them*—training. Nothing more. Nothing *real*. She knew *she* would never use her skills in actual battle and had let that permeate her thoughts on all the men's skills too.

But Abba had been struck down by an enemy dagger—in the back, at that. Kap was safeguarding against leaving a widow. Izik was looking at her as though she was a complete idiot for being taken by surprise by that offhanded statement, and she was afraid he might be right to think it. What sort of idiot girl didn't pause to wonder if it would take violence to take the Land from a violent people? Didn't pause to think that if she *did* choose a husband, she could lose him before they ever came into their inheritance?

Working a swallow past the sudden tightness in her chest, No'ah looked away from Izik, toward the bird still swooping overhead. "Kap may have the right idea, at that."

Izik snorted a disagreement. "Or he may die without ever knowing the joy of a wife. I'm not sure that's a trade *I* want to make."

The bird's circling made her dizzy. It must be the bird, not the thought of Izik with a wife.

No, it was Izik's fault. All Izik's fault. She sent him a pursed-lipped scowl. "So now you're wife hunting while we're husband hunting? Am I going to have spy on a few young women too, while we're at it? And who do you have in mind, anyway?"

She'd seen him making eyes at Keren a month or two ago—and Adi was one of the most beautiful women in all of Israel, everyone agreed about that, and was of age now. Had he set his sights on one of them?

She liked them both. She could imagine, when they all had houses of stone and vineyards and gardens, having celebrations and dinners with either of them, their children playing together. She just couldn't picture who her own husband would be or quite square the thought that Izik would be husband to one of them.

His boyish laugh, the same one he'd barked out all his life, didn't help solidify the thought of him taking one of them as a wife, either, or having children of his own. "Not Tirzah or Hoglah or Milcah, that's for sure."

That hardly narrowed it down. "Keren? Adi?"

He once again looked at her as though she were mad. "Keren's parents just arranged a betrothal with Noam. And Adi..." He wrinkled his nose.

She stiffened on her friend's behalf. "What wrong with Adi? She's even more beautiful than my sisters—or so I heard some of the boys saying a few months ago."

"Maybe, but she's...too delicate. She acts as if every stray spider is the next plague and every sneeze is going to be her death."

No'ah bit back a grin. Adi *did* tend toward exaggeration. She wasn't *actually* delicate, but it was true she acted like she was. "So you really don't have anyone in mind?"

He led the way back toward the wilderness, though they were far enough away from their tents now that the flock of wife-seeking men was out of view. "Just because I'm not inter- ested in Adi or Keren or your sisters, you think I have no par- ticular interest? You need to leave your tent more, Little Bee. There are far more young women in Israel than those few."

She left her tent more than any other young woman she knew, which meant she could laugh at that statement without feeling the slightest sting. "Who then?"

His grin said he didn't mean to tell her. "Someone prettier than Adi. And less annoying. Someone far better suited to me than any of your sisters."

"Sarah?"

He shot her a look. "I said *prettier*. And *less* annoying. And *better* suited to me."

She again huffed on behalf of a friend. And again laughed at his expression. Whoever had caught his eye, he really was smitten, if he thought whoever-she-was was so far superior to her dearest friends and sisters. "Be mysterious, then. I'll sort it out eventually."

"I have no doubt you will. Eventually. But *my* match is hardly the most pressing right now." He pointed ahead of them, and No'ah only noticed that a man strode some distance before them, clearly aimed toward the sheepfold belonging to Manasseh. She squinted to try to find some identifying feature in the near silhouette made by the setting sun. "Hoglah was looking quite closely at him yesterday."

"Who is it?"

"Asher."

"Ah." Hoglah had been looking quite closely at Asher for longer than that. No'ah hadn't even realized their cousin—son of the third of Abba's brothers—had been one of the masses at their door though. "You don't think *he* has secrets, do you? Because spying on him out here will be a challenge, unless you think he'll share his deepest, darkest thoughts with his sheep."

"He may, at that." But Izik was laughing. And shaking his head. "No, he just requires a bit of…direction, I think. Because he was looking at the wrong sister yesterday."

No'ah frowned. "Which of them was he looking at?" Hoglah would be devastated if Asher chose Tirzah or Milcah instead of her. She'd fancied him since well before Abba's death and had been all anxious nerves anytime rumor speculated on whether his parents were in negotiation with another girl's.

"You."

"What?" She stumbled over a rock—or so she told herself, because admitting there was no physical excuse for the trip was too embarrassing—and steadied herself with a hand to Izik's arm.

"You know, Little Bee, if you weren't constantly buzzing around trying to fix everything for everyone else, you may actually notice what relates to *you*."

She waved that away. "It *doesn't* relate to me. I could never consider Asher. Not as long as Hoglah's pining for him, certainly."

"Hence the redirection."

And how was it that *he* was so good at noticing all these things? She might have asked—and teased about how much attention he was paying to potential romance all of a sudden—had they not been catching up to Asher quickly, now that he'd slowed as he neared his sheep.

She tugged Izik into a slower pace. "And what's the plan for convincing him of this? Do I act obnoxious? Or is this a case of letting him see my true self, which will scare him away anyway?"

Izik's lips twitched. "How do you feel about sheep?"

The wrinkling of her nose was involuntary. "They're smelly and loud and stupid, and the week Abba made me train as a shepherdess was the worst of my life."

"There you go. Come on." He picked up speed again, even calling out a greeting to Asher after a few more steps.

Their cousin spun around with a smile for Izik that only grew when he spotted her beside him—which she *noticed*, thank you very much. Since Izik had pointed it out, anyway. She kept her own smile vague and easy...and made no attempt to hide her natural reaction, the closer they drew to the sheep.

It wasn't that she didn't appreciate the wealth of a herd—Abba had cultivated theirs with care and affection, and the result had been a notable increase. It wasn't that she didn't appreciate the wool that could be spun into fabric—the Israelites' clothing might not have worn out as they wandered, but the number of Israelites had grown over the last forty years, and new children still needed new material to dress in. It wasn't even that she couldn't recognize the sweetness of newborn lambs—the littlest ones in the sheepfold caught her eye even now and made her smile go a little more genuine.

It was just that they grew into *sheep*. Smelly, noisy, stupid *sheep*.

Izik was right. This redirection wouldn't be difficult at all—Hoglah was the shepherdess in the family, after all.

CHAPTER SEVEN

orty days. How had it already been forty days since the world ripped apart? Mahlah didn't have her bowl in her hands—she wasn't out here to collect the manna gathering like dew on the grass even now. As the sun crested the horizon and sent its rainbow of light through the sky, she made her way along the path she hadn't taken for over a month, to the last place in the world she'd imagined coming again.

The boulder hunched over the landscape, marking the spot where Abba had fallen. She wanted to see it as a looming monster, a dark blot on the landscape, a symbol of all that was threatening and uncertain and dangerous. She'd expected to want to pull her bow forward, have her dagger at the ready.

But the sun stretched its fingers out, caressed the giant slab, and teased colors to the surface visible at no other time of day. She saw the sparkle and glint of quartz in its veins, whispering of promise and light. And instead of the visible reminder of all she'd lost, she remembered *why* Abba had always come here to pray. Why this, ever since they first set up camp outside Shittim, had been his favorite spot.

She climbed up the face of the boulder with more ease than she would ever admit to in mixed company, and she smiled, remembering how Abba had called her his little mountain goat when she was a girl, until Imma had scolded him out of the habit. With the long limbs she'd inherited from him, climbing had always come naturally, and though she didn't do it now as often as she once had, her fingers and toes hadn't forgotten how to find the crevices in the face of the rock or the crooks in a trunk of a tree.

Within two minutes, she was perched on the top of the boulder, face toward the rising sun. She'd expected tears to keep her company today, the day that marked the end of their official time of mourning. Instead, her breath caught in familiar awe as she watched the Lord paint His wonders in the sky. Daybreak after daybreak, He reminded them of who He was.

The rock was still night-cool beneath her palms, but she leaned back onto them anyway, tilted her face toward the sun, and drew in a deep breath. The bulk of her day would be spent as it always was, tending the household chores and her sisters, making certain their flocks were well, making the pottery and beadwork that they would sell if ever they ventured back into a trade city. On top of that, now, was the sifting of suitors eager to gain the attention of her sisters.

No'ah had become a veritable fount of information on them all, and Mahlah had decided not to ask how she was learning all she was. She'd simply accept the knowledge and use it and be grateful.

No doubt today, like every day lately, the sisters would gather for the noon meal and discuss their options. The younger ones would sigh wistfully over who had paid them a visit the day before, who was the handsomest, the kindest, the strongest, the bravest. Mahlah would add what she knew about their families. No'ah would share anything she'd discovered about their habits or complaints or expectations. Some would be dismissed. Others would be welcomed for another visit.

All good things. Necessary things. But not what she wanted to think about this morning. This morning, she wanted to watch the sunrise bathe the earth in color, to hear the birds waking to their songs, to smell freshly fallen manna and the gurgling river nearby, and to know that the world went on, despite the ache deep inside. The world went on, and she would too. Because God was still her God, and He was the Lord of the living.

All these forty days, she'd been remembering this spot as where Abba fell—where his life was taken. But sitting here now, she saw it for what it really was: Abba's favorite place. The one where He'd last praised the Lord. Though his blood had stained the ground, his worship had painted the air here.

The sun climbed higher, its rainbow fading to brilliant gold, its heat increasing with each degree it rose. The camp awoke, sounds of movement filtering into the morning. Mahlah drew in a deep breath, knowing it would be the last moment of quiet she'd have until the sun set again and she crawled into bed.

"Abba…" She knew he wasn't here, though she didn't know where exactly his soul had flown. She didn't know if, wherever his spirit rested, he could still hear her. She only knew that *she* still had words she needed to say to him. And if the Lord was God of the living, and He was most assuredly Abba's God, then surely it meant that her father's soul still lived somewhere, with the Lord. She would cling to that hope.

"Abba, forty days aren't enough to mourn you. Forty *years* may not be." She watched a flock of birds rise up from the south, wing their way east, across the blinding face of the sun. "You were a father who taught us more than what was expected of us—you taught us how to *live*. How to love God. How to seek a life worth singing about. I don't think we ever truly appreciated that until you were gone. But now, with all that has followed—now we see it so clearly."

She paused, listened to the voice of the wind for a moment, sighed. "It was always enough for us to be your daughters—but only with you gone do we see what that really means. That's what they're calling us now, you know: the Five Daughters. The whole camp has taken up your favorite hymn and calls it 'The Shadow's Song.' They talk about us as though we're something special, but...but we know it isn't us. It was *you*. You were so special. You were so deserving. You were so worthy." Her lips quivered as she smiled. "So thank you. Because if *we* are anything good, anything noble, anything worth seeking, it is only because we're your daughters."

Her words ran dry, but her heart didn't. It pulsed with all the things that went beyond words—the sorrow, the gratitude, the missing of him, the awareness of how deeply he remained in all that mattered most, in the very fabric of her being.

After a few minutes more, she heaved out a long breath and decided that the figures leaving camp and heading for the herds meant it was time to climb down, gather the day's manna, and get to work. Scrambling down was always a bit harder than getting up, in her opinion, and certainly required her full attention. That was why, when she turned to face the camp again, she started at finding a male form only a few steps away. She hadn't even time to reach for her weapon before recognition came.

Uriel looked no less surprised at finding *her* out here. "Mahlah?" His eyes flew over the surroundings, his brows knit. "Do you really think it's safe to be out here alone? In the very place where…? We *know* there are bandits out here."

Had the words come from Cozbi, she would have chafed under them. From Uriel, they sounded merely concerned for her welfare. Her cheeks heated, and she pulled forward the small bow and quiver of arrows that had been half hidden by her braid. "I wasn't careless. Nor so lost in my prayers as Abba could be."

"I would never call you careless—or helpless. I've seen your aim with that bow." A smile flitted over his lips, his words calling to mind the day two weeks ago when she, Uriel, Kapriel, Izik, and No'ah all went out together to check on their families' cattle and had taken the opportunity for some target practice. Kap and Iz were both used to her aim putting theirs to shame, but Uriel had been flatteringly impressed. "Even so, I would feel better if you didn't come out here alone so early."

He cared. Most people did in passing, but his tone sounded far more than *passing*, and it pulled her a step closer to his side. "I wouldn't usually, but…it's the fortieth day. I had to…I just…"

"Ah. I'd lost count." He reached out, or she did, or both of them, and their fingers tangled together. "I would have risked

91

it too, then." A beat of silence, a squeeze of his fingers. "I wish I'd had the chance to know him better. I wish…I wish I'd spoken a day sooner. A week. A month."

Her lips quirked up. "We'd only met a month before."

"But I knew the moment I set eyes on you that you were the one I wanted to pursue. I should have gone that very hour to meet your father." A corner of his mouth tugged higher than its counterpart. "My mother always calls it the curse of youth, thinking we have all the time in the world and hence never making good use of it."

Had he really known that immediately, like Jacob with Rachel? Her chest thrummed at the thought. She'd always thought herself too practical to be involved in anything like that—that if anything, she'd be the Leah in an arrangement, the elder daughter holding the others back. Not the one someone would fall in love with at first glance.

Though he'd been visiting every day, she'd yet to meet his family. His mother, she knew, had a knee injury that kept her from walking far, and his father had died not long after they arrived at their current camp, though she didn't know of what. When she could get away from the busyness of her own house, she would have to see if Keturah would go with her to meet his imma. If they really did mean to talk about a betrothal, it was only fitting.

She flushed again at the very thought. "I wish Abba had known you too. He could always see straight to a person's heart, and I know he would have liked you."

The way Uriel's cheeks reddened and his gaze shifted away made her grin. At least she wasn't the only one who blushed at

the thought of meeting the other's parents. "I know—his reputation preceded him. And it may have been part of why I
hesitated. I was certain he'd take one look at me and declare
I wasn't good enough for his oldest daughter. I'm not even of
your tribe."

She chuckled. "That wouldn't have mattered to him. You're
part of Israel, not a pagan—*that's* all he cared about."

He didn't look convinced. "Really?"

"Well. Perhaps not *all*." She could hear No'ah voice listing
all the marks against their many suitors—marks Abba would
have pointed out too, no doubt. "But he'd have liked you. He
wasn't the sort to dislike anyone I looked overlong at. He was
anxious for me to…to find someone I cared about so deeply.
Who cared for me in turn."

They'd eased closer, somehow. She couldn't have said
when. But when he lifted his free hand and trailed his fingers
down her cheek, then followed her braid down her back and
rested it against her waist, she found herself leaning even
closer. "I do care," he whispered. His eyes were locked on hers.
"The more I learn of you, Mahlah, the more I find to love.
Especially now, in these hard times. Seeing how you honor
your father's memory, fight for his legacy, care for your sisters—
your heart is as beautiful as your face."

"What's going on here? You—unhand her at once!"

It was the ferocity of the voice more than the words themselves that had Mahlah and Uriel leaping apart, both turning
to face whoever had come upon them. Mahlah nearly reached
for her bow, but recognition halted her.

Perhaps she halted too soon, though, because in the next moment Cozbi was upon them, his face blank rage, and he grabbed hold of Mahlah's arm so fiercely she cried out in startled pain and tried to pull free.

He yanked her hard, hard enough to send her behind him. "You Benjaminite scum! How dare you accost a daughter of Manasseh?"

"Accost?" Uriel had backed up a step, hands raised, palms out, to show he had no weapon or bad intentions. "Cozbi, calm yourself. We were only talking, there was nothing untoward going on."

"*Talking?*" Cozbi still hadn't let go of her arm, but now that Mahlah had regained her balance, anger was elbowing out the surprise and pain, even when he gave her a shake. "That didn't look like *talking.*"

She grabbed Cozbi's offending wrist with her opposite one, squeezing hard enough to steal his attention. No doubt the way she snarled at him would convince him that she was far from the most attractive of the Five Daughters—fine by her. "Take your hand off me this instant, Cozbi, or I will demonstrate every last move Abba taught me about how to defend myself against unwanted male advances."

Cozbi made a show of releasing her, holding his own palms up and out, but it looked mocking when paired with his sneer. "Oh, that's right. Your mighty father taught you all manner of unwomanly things. So tell me then, *cousin*, why weren't you fending off the advances of *that* half-breed? He isn't even fully Israelite!"

She'd been about to say that Uriel's advances weren't unwanted, but that last bit stayed her words. She looked to Uriel, whose cheeks were flushed again. In anger this time, given the glint of his eyes.

His hands had curled into fists at his side. "My mother renounced the heritage of her birth and was fully adopted into the People long before she married my father. She is a loyal servant of the Lord."

Defensiveness wove a tapestry through his tone, with threads of fury and something else flashing through. Guilt? It sounded like it, looked like it. But he had no reason to feel guilty for the blood his mother had been born with—on the contrary, if she had abandoned her own culture in favor of service to the One True God, she deserved credit for that. And Uriel should be proud of her.

But defending oneself all one's life against such implications must wear on a person. Make him resentful, even guilty for what he couldn't help.

Certainly it would make him hesitate to speak to the father of a girl who'd caught his attention...especially one like *hers*.

Sweet Uriel. Now she was even more determined to meet his mother.

And to put Cozbi in his place. She pivoted, put herself between them, and planted her hands on her waist. "Enough! You may be a tribesman, Cozbi, but you—"

"Silence! Upstart woman—how is it you don't know your place?" The way Cozbi charged at her, she thought for a second that he was going to strike her. But no, he simply grabbed her arm again and again tried the swinging move—only this time she was ready and dug in her heels.

She probably could have then upset his balance and landed him flat on his back, but he barked out, "Kapriel! If you don't get her under control, I'm going to report her to the elders!"

Kapriel? Her gaze flew past Uriel, and for the first time she actually took note of the others with him—and more running up, drawn by the commotion.

Danijel stood still enough to say he'd been there for a while already, along with Cozbi's younger brother. Kapriel and Izik were rushing up, their father a few paces behind them, looking cross…though she couldn't say at whom it was aimed.

When Kap hurried directly to her side, sent a look over his shoulder toward Uriel—an apology?—and urged her to the side, out of the way, she went. "What's going on?" Kap breathed in her ear, too softly to be heard over Cozbi.

"Seth!" Cozbi was shouting. "You can bear witness. I found that girl in the arms of this half-pagan Benjaminite. It isn't to be borne!"

Mahlah huffed out a breath. "I was out here remembering Abba. Uriel was concerned when he saw me alone, and we were talking. That's all."

It might not have been, had no one come upon them. He might have kissed her—and she certainly would have let him. But that was no crime, especially given that he'd declared his intentions.

Kap sighed. "Abba, you don't need to scowl like that. Uriel is seeking a betrothal. Mahlah was only waiting until the end of her mourning period to make her decision known, but we all know what's coming."

"What?" Cozbi seethed now, rage not just blanketing his face but boiling up into his eyes. "No. You can't. You can't marry someone from a whole other *tribe!*"

When she failed to give him any reaction other than a long blink, Cozbi spun to face her uncle. "Tell her! If she marries someone from another tribe, then that man will end up with part of Manasseh's inheritance!"

Seth's brow furrowed in a way she knew too well. A way that said someone had made a point he didn't like but couldn't refute. Usually she saw that look on his face when Izik was lobbying for something that didn't seem quite wise but he couldn't put his finger on why. It was strange, seeing it on her uncle's face here, in response to Cozbi.

Seth made a calming gesture with his arms. "Easy, Cozbi. You do no one any credit with your outbursts, and your handling of Mahlah is unacceptable."

"Me?" Cozbi laughed, but it sounded more like a shout to her ears than any sign of mirth. "You'll take fault with *me?*" He backed away a step, sending his scathing glare across Mahlah and Kapriel, then Uriel, and back to Seth. "I supported the petition to Moses because I thought the Five Daughters would have the good sense to think it through and marry within the tribe—something you all would have made sure of if *you'd* been making the decisions. But if they're going to be bargaining away our land for mere affection that will pass like the wind anyway, then it's time to take matters into our own hands."

He strode away, Danijel falling in beside him. Not until they were halfway back to camp did Mahlah actually draw in a breath deep enough to calm her.

Kapriel let one out and rubbed a hand over his face. "Well. That was an exciting start to the morning." Somehow, he managed a smile. It was a little crooked, but it was there. "Everyone all right?"

Mahlah nodded, even though her arm still ached enough where Cozbi had grabbed her that she suspected he'd left a bruise. If she pointed it out, though, she knew well that her cousins would chase after him and return the favor, and she'd just as soon not give him any more fuel to add to the fire of his anger. "What do you think he'll do?"

"Talk to the elders, no doubt." Seth pinched the bridge of his nose. "You'd better get back to camp, Mahlah, and tell Abiram about this, since he's the one who's taken charge of all the potential matches. You know how little he likes surprises."

She did. But the certainty that she'd done nothing wrong made her no more eager to tell another uncle about the encounter. Still, what could she do but nod? "I will."

"I'll walk you back," Uriel said, taking a step toward her in proof.

Izik's brows flew toward his hairline. "Are you certain that's a wise idea?"

Uriel's face hardened. "I'm walking her back."

Iz held his hands up in surrender. But he shot a look toward Kapriel. She half expected him to insist he'd come along too—and she would have let him, probably—but he nodded instead.

A moment later, she and Uriel were on the path back toward camp, and a moment after that, her tent was in view again. Silence walked beside them through those moments, and she had to wonder if the same thoughts were catapulting through his mind that were in hers.

They'd nearly reached home again when he finally said, "Will you meet my mother? I don't…I'm not ashamed of her. I wasn't hiding her. But I didn't know how you'd react."

She offered him a smile she hoped put his fears to rest. "I'd love to. I'll bring Keturah with me." He would understand that bringing her mother's sister was the closest she could come to bringing her own imma to meet his. Bridging their two families. Building a connection. "Today?"

His shoulders relaxed, and his handsome smile turned his lips up and brought the dimples to his cheeks. "I'll go and tell her to expect you…after the midday meal? I can meet you here, walk you there."

Given that she had no idea where his tent was, that sounded wise. She nodded. "I'll be waiting."

CHAPTER EIGHT

No'ah had been a spy for only a few weeks, but she and Izik joked regularly now about how well suited they would be for the task, if Moses and Joshua opted to send more scouts into the Promised Land before they marched on it. She had made such a habit of slipping out of the tent over the years anyway that her sisters thought nothing of her regular disappearances. And she'd "buzzed about" the camp so regularly, as Iz put it, that no one thought anything of the two of them doing so now too.

Even today, in broad daylight. She didn't earn a single questioning look as she trailed Cozbi, Danijel, and half a dozen other tribesmen toward where Simon sat outside on his favorite cushion, telling stories to the little ones and whittling a pipe that looked much like Kapriel's. "I wonder where Zelig is?" she muttered to Izik. Of the suitors they'd discovered to be more concerned with their inheritance than with the sisters, only he was missing from the knot around Cozbi.

"His father sent him to the far pastures today." Izik touched a hand to the small of her back to nudge her to the right, around another tent to keep them out of view of the disgruntled men once they stopped at Simon's. "How did Abiram react?"

No'ah winced at the very thought. "He got very quiet." Which meant he was upset. *Very* upset. "Especially when

Mahlah showed him the bruises on her arm where Cozbi grabbed her."

"The *what*?" Izik came to a halt beside her, spinning to send a rather angry-looking gaze down on her himself. "She didn't say he'd hurt her!"

And when No'ah had realized he had, she'd nearly gone storming off to do some damage to him herself—but she understood why Mahlah had chosen silence instead, and she made a point now of patting Izik's arm and smiling reassuringly. She hoped. "He didn't really. It's just a little bruise on her arm, no worse that we all get all the time by bumping into things."

The point remained, of course, that this one hadn't been the result of an accident or carelessness. It had been the result of a cruel-hearted, selfish man who thought he had the right to treat Mahlah however he pleased.

As if his actions would ever, *ever* convince any of them to choose *him* as a husband.

Izik didn't look mollified, but he set it aside and continued toward Simon's tent. Or close to it, anyway. He stopped her at the corner of the neighboring home, where they remained out of view of the gathering men, but within earshot.

Simon was even now greeting them all by name, asking after their parents and siblings, their nieces and nephews. No'ah didn't much care about the niceties, so she instead made herself comfortable on the ground and pulled out the embroidery she'd been working on. She hadn't said as much aloud, but she meant it to be for Mahlah's wedding garments. And she'd brought her handwork out to random parts of camp often enough over the years that, again, no one would think it odd—just fidgeting No'ah escaping the prying eyes of her family again and choosing a random spot to do her work.

Izik lowered himself to the ground beside her, pulling out his own handwork—a wood block and his knife, though he hadn't enough of a start for her to know what he meant to make of it.

Cozbi had apparently had enough of the niceties too. He interrupted Simon's next query about someone's sister with, "It isn't to be borne, Simon. You must do something, you and the other elders."

Was it her imagination, or did Simon sigh? Perhaps it was just the wind. "I need a bit more clarification, Cozbi."

"The Five Daughters! Or the First, at any rate." The way Cozbi's voice got louder and softer made her think he was pacing in front of Simon, probably slicing a hand through the air or waving it around like a madman. Or so she saw him in her mind's eye. "She's considering a betrothal to a Benjaminite!"

If Simon made an immediate response, she couldn't hear it. Perhaps he hummed or simply leaned back to consider. At length he said, "Well, the tribe of Benjamin is a respectable one. Benjamin and Joseph, after all, were the two—"

"I'm not concerned with the history," Cozbi snapped. Usually, cutting off an elder mid-reminiscence was considered a grave misconduct. Had a child done such a thing, his mother or father would have scolded him fiercely and sent him to bed. Cozbi, however, just pushed on. "I'm concerned with the *future*. Mahlah stands to inherit as much as a firstborn son—not just of her father's flocks and herds, but *land*."

"I'm aware," Simon said, voice mild.

"Land that, if she marries outside the tribe, will then leave our tribal lands and be given to another. Think about that—a sizeable portion of Manasseh, handed to Benjamin."

This time Simon's sigh filtered around the tent corner to her without trouble. He followed it with "Oh."

Oh. A world of meaning in one little syllable. She could practically hear the epiphany settling on him.

No'ah pulled her needle and thread through the cloth but then went still. If she were being completely honest, she saw their point too. She did. It was a wrinkle in inheritance that had never come up for her people before, as they'd never had land to pass down from generation to generation. But as they all thought it through, ramifications compounded.

Give land to your sons, and it remains in the tribe forever. But give it to a daughter who marries elsewhere...and then what?

No'ah blustered out a breath. It would have been easier had Mahlah simply fallen in love with Kapriel or Danijel or Adam or Reboahim. There was no shortage of good, kind, handsome men in Manasseh. Why had it been Uriel to catch her eye? Her heart?

Not that she would ever say such a thing out loud. Wherever Mahlah stood, No'ah would stand beside her. They were sisters.

"That...does pose a disturbing possibility. Perhaps if he were of Ephraim, still part of the split tribe of Joseph...but Benjamin?"

"We can't allow a portion of our land to be promised to another tribe before we even take control of it." Another voice this time. It was familiar, but she couldn't readily place which of the half dozen men it was. "It isn't right. I was supportive of giving the Five Daughters an inheritance, but there need to be rules. Stipulations."

"They cannot be allowed to marry outside the tribe." Cozbi again.

"I...do see your point."

So did No'ah, but that didn't mean she liked what it meant for her family. No other daughters in Israel had such a stipulation put on them. People married between their tribes all the time—Izik and Kapriel's mother had been of the tribe of Naphtali, and Cozbi's own was from Zebulun. When it only meant walking a little farther across the camp to visit one's siblings or parents, that was no great thing.

But it would be different when they were spread out across the Promised Land. She knew that. Just as she knew that having their own inheritance made it different for them too.

She looked over at Izik, whose knife had stilled on his block. He stared out at nothing, his jaw set. For a moment, idly, as a distraction from the more pressing matter, she wondered what tribe the girl he'd set his heart on was from. But it flitted away again—it wouldn't impact his ability to marry her, whoever she was. Not like this could do for them.

Simon sighed so loudly she heard it even here. "I will speak to the other elders. I think...I think we'll have to take this concern to Moses and see what he says. I don't feel comfortable dictating to the Daughters whom they must marry, when their uncles have already given them permission to chose their own husbands. If such a pronouncement is going to limit their choices, then it must come from the Lord, not us."

No'ah let her head sag. She had a sinking feeling that she knew what Moses would say.

"What?" It should have appeased Cozbi, shouldn't it have? But he sounded more outraged than ever. "There's no need to bother the leader with it—you can put restrictions in place, you're the senior elder, our tribe's judge—"

"And this is concerning a decision that came through Moses from God Himself. Who am I to add to or take away from it? No. We'll go to Moses."

"But—"

"Enough!" Simon's tone made No'ah start. She'd never actually heard him sound so firm and unyielding, though of course she knew that with all the tribe's decisions he made, he must be when the situation required it. It had just never happened around her. "The first decision was for all of Israel, not just the tribe of Manasseh—and so, if there is a clarification, *it* will concern all of Israel too. This is outside my purview. Either be satisfied that the Lord will speak the best good, Cozbi, or make it clear to everyone assembled here that your motives are selfish."

She couldn't hear any response from Cozbi, though a general murmur followed Simon's pronouncement as the gathered men wondered over what Moses would say—and at least one voice laughed quietly about how Cozbi would be refused by the Five Daughters anyway, so why was he so determined?

He must have stomped off already, for one of his companions to have said that.

She looked over at Izik, ready to make a joke that agreed with the sentiment, but Iz's face was dark with contemplation. Serious enough that she frowned in response. "What is it?"

"Cozbi. He may be a donkey, but he's no fool. He has to *know* that none of you would choose him freely as a husband, so…why is he so determined?"

"Tribal loyalty?" It was the best answer she had. She shoved her embroidery back into the small bag she wore slung over her torso.

Izik stood, held out a hand for her, and pulled her to her feet. Her answer didn't ease his serious expression any. "Let's hope it's only that."

She caught the end of her braid in her hand and wound it around her wrist. "What else could it be?"

Somehow, his face went even darker. "There are ways to force a woman to marry you—ways the Law demands. You know as well as I that it has come up a time or two over the years."

"You don't mean…you can't think he'd force himself on one of us." But of course that was what he meant. The Law had been designed to protect women who had been attacked, to make their attackers care for them for life after they'd made them undesirable to other men. But it was a Law that weighed more heavily on the victim than the guilty party. She did, in fact, know one woman married to the man who had taken her innocence by violence. She spent most of her days hidden away inside the tent and rarely spoke when out with the other women. She looked…haunted. Empty.

Izik's face was hard as stone. "Tell your sisters not to go anywhere alone. Especially Mahlah. And never leave home without your weapons. Take them everywhere. All the time. Even in camp. And whenever possible, make sure you don't go out alone either. All right?"

It wasn't a question, just as it wasn't an order—not the kind those men back there would make. It was wisdom, given with urgency from one friend to another. Pulse thrumming, No'ah nodded. "All right. We'll be careful. And never alone."

It chafed, she could admit that. She loved solitude as much as she loved manna cakes drizzled with honey. But finding herself forced into a marriage with someone like Cozbi would chafe far more.

A shiver coursed through her, and she moved a little closer than usual to Izik as they turned back toward home. "I'm beginning to think this edict isn't the blessing it first appeared."

Iz slung an arm over her shoulders. "It will be. Once you're all safely married."

They reached the end of the row of tents, and No'ah spotted Mahlah and Keturah striding through the main thoroughfare, heading out of Manasseh and toward Benjamin, baskets in both their arms. Going, she knew, to meet Uriel's widowed mother.

Her throat went tight. She'd thought one of them, at least, would soon be safely betrothed and then married, happy and safe and settled. But Cozbi might yet snatch that away from Mahlah. "At least Asher and Hoglah may survive this, since Asher is a cousin. And smiling at the right sister now." That would only leave Milcah and Tirzah to find happiness for, and she had a few solid contenders in mind after all her observation. Their cousin Micah and Milcah had been getting along splendidly—and saying their names together was halfway to a song. For Tirzah...gracious, she couldn't make up her mind. Tirzah got along with *everybody*, and everybody with her. She needed someone who would keep her brightness shining, who would encourage and cherish her. Eldad, maybe. Or Chanoch.

Izik finally chuckled, the sound breaking the tension that had been holding his arm too taut. He relaxed. "One sister safely matched."

"We hope."

"We hope. Four to go."

Right. Four. She always forgot to include herself in her mental calculations. It was enough to make her sigh again. "I really don't need to be in love with my husband at the start. A good man will suffice. Maybe I'll just convince your brother to put aside his notions of fighting first."

That had Izik jerking away, his eyes first going wide and then narrowing on her. "You had better be joking, Little Bee."

She was. Mostly. She couldn't imagine marrying Kap—but then, she couldn't imagine marrying anyone. Still, Izik's reaction had been enough to bring her usual good humor bubbling back up, and it spilled out in a chuckle, punctuated by a grin. "Why? Don't you want me as a sister?"

"You would drive each other to madness in a fortnight. You know how he reacts to your buzzing. And how *you* react to his steadiness."

She did, which brought a new chuckle to her throat. "Abiram assures me that married couples adjust to each other. What first chafes comes to complement. They strengthen each other…or something like that."

"If they don't drive each other to complete madness first."

"All right, not Kapriel. So then maybe…" No names sprang to mind. No handsome faces begged for her to linger over them in her recollection. She sighed. "I have no idea. Do you?"

"Of course I do." He said it so simply, and with that easy, sure confidence he always had. Like nothing in the world could take him by surprise, throw him off his guard. He didn't even bother smiling, just urged her onto the path toward home.

"Wait—you do?" She pulled him to a halt with a huff. "And when are you going to tell me who it is?"

"When you're ready to hear it." He lifted his brows, the corners of his lips following them up. "Are you?"

For a moment, she imagined him saying a name, she imagined calling the face to mind, she imagined reviewing the virtues and faults of whoever it was. And imagined herself, too, running out into the wilderness and avoiding that name and face for the rest of her life, just out of principle. "No. Definitely not. Maybe after everyone else's future has been settled." Maybe then she'd be able to worry about her own.

Izik just chuckled, tugged on her braid to get her moving again, and faced forward. "That's what I thought."

CHAPTER NINE

There were strangers all throughout the camp of Israel—or people who began as strangers, anyway. There were Egyptians who had fled with them, people from the lands they'd gone through or conquered who had been won over by the One True God and had gone through the process of renouncing their former gods and countries and joining the people of the Lord.

Mahlah had seen many of them over the years, had spoken with them, and had thought very little about it otherwise. To her mind, anyone who turned to the Lord ought to receive a warm welcome, as sojourners who found their true home.

But then, she'd never found herself asking for entrance to the tent of a former stranger before, wondering if the woman who called out an invitation to come in would think her an appropriate bride for her only son. She'd never had to wonder what her own imma's sister would think of this potential new covenant uniting their families.

She had never had to wonder what her father would have said, had he lived to say it. Abba was a fair man, it was true. But he'd fought the enemies whose lands they'd passed through. He'd lost an uncle in the early battles after the Exodus. He could have harbored a bias that had simply never come up.

But the voice that called out a welcome was warm, sweet, and spoke in the familiar cadence of Mahlah's people. She stepped inside with Keturah at her side, knowing well that her smile would look as bashful as it felt. Not because Uriel's mother, Gila, had once been an Amorite, but because she was Uriel's *mother.*

"Thank you so much for allowing us to visit you," she said as she dipped her knees respectfully, her eyes searching the dim interior for the woman who had called out to them.

"It is an honor to be welcomed into your tent," Keturah added.

Mahlah finally spotted their hostess. She was pushing herself up from a seat with a great deal of effort, wincing as she straightened her right knee. Her face cleared as soon as she was upright though, and she beamed a smile. She approached slowly, but with hands outstretched. "Mahlah—and your mother's sister, Keturah. You cannot know the pleasure it brings my heart to finally meet you. Come, please! Sit—would you like some tea?"

They accepted the offer and offered in response the gifts they'd brought—a jar of honey, some berries that Keturah's children had gathered that morning, a few sticks of cinnamon.

Gila was a lovely woman—she looked a bit older than Keturah, probably near Imma's age. Uriel had already told Mahlah the story, that morning, of how she had ended up with the People. When the previous generation had gone to battle with the Amorites, she'd been only a girl—a girl who had always had a yearning in her heart for a god unlike the one her people told her about. She'd been orphaned a few months before the Israelites marched into her land, and when she heard the stories whispered in fear in the streets—stories of a God who parted the sea, who sent plagues upon Egypt, who did the impossible for His people out of love for them—she had simply acted on instinct.

She'd run straight from the city that had abandoned her, straight to the camp of the People who should have been her enemy. She'd thrown herself on the mercy of the first people she saw—an older couple of the tribe of Benjamin—and had begged them to take her in and teach her about this God she yearned to know. She'd told them everything she could about her city, though how helpful a child's view of it was, Uriel hadn't known.

Even so, she had been spared the annihilation the rest of her people had received. She'd been taught the ways of God, welcomed into His family, and even adopted by that couple who had first caught her up. She had never looked back.

Uriel had told the story hurriedly, looking over his shoulder, clearly looking for someone who would disapprove. "She doesn't speak of it much," he'd said at the end of the tale. "My father would ask her things all the time, but since he died..." He'd shaken his head. "She prefers not to speak of the past. It pains her."

She'd promised, of course, not to bring it up then. If Gila wanted to tell her story, Mahlah would be glad to hear it, but if not, then it was enough to know the facts from Uriel.

At the moment, Gila seemed more concerned with getting to know Mahlah than with rehashing her own history. She asked about Mahlah's family, what it was like to be the eldest of so many sisters, how she'd managed to raise them all when she was still so young when Imma had died.

There, she looked to Keturah, her lovely face kind and warm. "I imagine you helped her a lot at the beginning."

Keturah laughed. "Not as much as you may think. She was already helping my sister with all the household tasks, so there was little I could teach her—and I had only recently been married myself and was a bit occupied setting up my own household. Her abba's mother was still alive then and helped, as did her other aunts...but mostly, Mahlah just did what needed done. And she did it with love and a smile. That's Mahlah."

Mahlah's cheeks felt warm, though not like they had that morning. She'd been hearing her family's praise most of her life, and it had always been encouraging, edifying, but nothing she felt she needed to list as an accomplishment. Doing what needed to be done, with joy that one was able to do it, was nothing special, was it? Everyone did it. Well, perhaps not always with the joy. But raising her sisters brought that on its own, along with a healthy dose of frustrating moments and plenty when she despaired of ever doing the right thing for them.

Gila sent her smile back to Mahlah. "My Uriel describes you as strong, selfless, overflowing with all things good. I can see already what he saw when you were first introduced." She leaned closer, her eyes sparkling much like his did. "I knew it the day he met you, you know. When he came home, something was...different. He had a bounce in his step I'd never seen. I knew a young woman was responsible—though it took me weeks to wheedle it out of him." She laughed, a full-throated, free laugh. "Sons don't like to share such things with their mothers—but I prevailed."

Keturah laughed along with her. "How well I know that. My boys are only six, but already they shy away from any talk of things of the heart."

Her laugh gradually dying down to a chuckle, Gila shook her head. "I was so glad when he made friends with Kapriel and Izik—good young men, those two. And all the gladder when it meant he met *you*. You have brought a light back to his eyes that had been missing since his father died."

Mahlah smiled, but it was small and tight, given the mentioned loss. "He hasn't spoken much of his abba. I only know he died a year ago."

Gila nodded, sobering. It didn't look quite like the grief Mahlah knew too well. It was…careful. "Betzalel was not always an easy man, not for either of us to live with. He was…restless. Never happy with what we had. I sometimes wondered…" She paused, averted her face, even closed her eyes. "I have never said this to anyone, and perhaps I shouldn't say it to you either. But if my son means to make you family, then perhaps you can know."

The air felt heavy, thick. Mahlah leaned forward, feeling as though her every word had to tiptoe. "You can tell me anything you want to, Gila. I will honor your confidence."

The woman drew in a long breath. "I wondered if perhaps his death was part of the Lord's purging of the faithless—he never served Him wholly. He thought Him cruel, capricious, thought His Law burdensome." She shook her head, but it only served to send a teardrop tracking down her cheek. She wiped it away. "I tried to show him how good the Lord is, but who was I, that he would listen to me?"

"His wife," Keturah said, voice calm and strong.

"A woman who had chosen the Lord of her own volition," Mahlah added. "You were probably able to show him the Lord's truth better than anyone else could have. It is too easy to take for granted the Truth with which you're raised."

Gila wiped at the other cheek too. "And I told myself many times over the years that perhaps that was why he was chosen as my husband. Perhaps the Lord would use me to reach him. Perhaps I could help him see that Truth. Though I am not certain I ever succeeded."

What a hard thing. Mahlah had no wisdom to offer, certainly no assurances. All she could do was reach across the gap between them and take Gila's hand. "We can never know such things. But we can trust. And you can know too that your story isn't over. You can take comfort in the son the Lord has given you."

Gila smiled through her tears and sniffed, squeezing Mahlah's fingers. "You're right. Uriel is a good boy. I worried, for a while, that he would be too influenced by Betzalel, but... but he is his own man. Far different from his father. He will be a good husband."

"Sometimes it is the very influence we most fear that turns our loved ones onto the right path." Keturah punctuated this with a nod. "My brother was caught up with a bad crowd for a while, and our mother feared for him fiercely. But it was seeing the path those others ended up on that steered Elyakim back to the Lord."

Nodding along with her, Gila reclaimed her fingers with a smile for Mahlah and wiped away the last of her tears. "I am glad of that, for your family's sake. And glad that Uriel too is on the path he's on. That he has good friends now. And a beautiful, strong woman who has captured his heart."

Perhaps eventually, hearing such things wouldn't make her own heart patter, wouldn't make her pulse skid, wouldn't make her lips quirk and quiver, searching for a shape they didn't know how to make—something more than a smile, that would hold in all the joy threatening to overflow her heart but still express it.

Perhaps eventually, but that day wasn't today.

They visited for a while longer, and then Keturah motioned that it was time for them to leave so she could get home before she needed to prepare their evening meal. Gila stood with them, drew Mahlah into an embrace, and held her there for a long moment. "I will be honored to call you daughter," she whispered into Mahlah's ear. "As soon as it can be arranged."

Mahlah couldn't decide whether to thank her or to return the sentiment, saying something about what a blessing it would be to have an imma again. So she simply gave Gila a squeeze and, when she pulled away, a smile. That must have said what she needed it to, because Gila looked happy as could be as she bade them farewell.

The day was still sunny and bright outside, and Mahlah would have sworn the birds all sang a little louder overhead as they started back toward Manasseh's tents.

Keturah looped their arms together and smiled up at her. "That went well, I'd say."

Mahlah nodded, unable to restrain her smile. "She's lovely."

"She is. And no doubt lonely enough, with only one son who must be about his business all day. She'll be very grateful to have a daughter join her family, and will take joy in any grandchildren that come along."

Mahlah nodded. Some of her friends had expressed concern before their marriages—and occasionally after them—that they would clash with their husband's mother, that there would be tension and fighting over control. But Mahlah was well accustomed to balancing the needs of multiple women under one roof. She liked to think she could navigate that new dimension as well as she had learned to balance the needs of her sisters. "Do you think…how soon do you think Abiram will allow a betrothal covenant to be drawn up? I know he wants us all to take our time and choose carefully, but this is what I want. Uriel is the man I love."

Keturah bumped their shoulders together, grinning. "I'll talk to him. I'm certain we can bring him around. And it isn't as though he hasn't been learning all he can about his family already. Had he any objections, he would have raised them before now."

It was true. Abiram liked Uriel, just as Kapriel and Izik did. As the rest of her uncles did. As Abba would have done. As everyone but Cozbi seemed to—and he didn't count.

Why had she even let herself think about him? It made her arm hurt again and dimmed her joy a bit, at least around the edges. But then, she ought to be grateful to him. His behavior this morning had spurred Uriel to arrange for her to meet his mother. If anything, he'd hurried their relationship along. And how furious would *that* thought make him?

They filled the rest of the walk with what a wedding ceremony could look like, reminiscing plenty about Keturah's and the other cousins' and friends' they'd attended since. There was, of course, the possibility that her sisters could be celebrating marriages at the same or similar times too—Hoglah and Asher seemed to be on that course, for sure. There were several young men that could be good matches for Milcah and Tirzah…though No'ah. Mahlah bit her lip and chuckled over the thought of No'ah ever settling enough to choose a husband. "She may well be the last of us to make a choice."

Keturah laughed. "I suspect she wants it that way. And perhaps after everyone else is settled, she'll be able to focus on herself. Fewer things to distract her then."

And she was clearly enjoying this part—every time she shared something she'd learned about a suitor, she had a gleam of satisfaction in her eyes. Mahlah nodded.

Her family's tent was just ahead of them now, and Keturah was reclaiming her arm so they could part ways. But Kapriel stepped out of the tent, spotted her, and strode toward them with enough purpose that they both went still. Mahlah's smile froze at the look on his face, and her hands fell to her sides. "What? What is it?"

He glanced at Keturah but then back to her. "You've been summoned by Moses. All of you. You're to come at once."

CHAPTER TEN

H ow many times could the world shift before they all were reduced to rubble? No'ah stood beside Mahlah once more in Moses's tent, but this time her fingers were curled into her palms, part fist and part desperate plea.

Please, Lord God. She had no offering, no priest to send up the prayer for her, no idea what the proper form for this request even was. She knew only that it pounded from her heart with every beat. *Have mercy. Have mercy on us. On her. She deserves happiness.*

She shifted until her arm just touched Mahlah's—a point of connection, a reminder for them both that they were in this together. Both of them. All of them. Even if Mahlah was the only one of them whose heart was at stake here today, she wasn't alone. No'ah prayed her older sister knew that, that she could feel No'ah's support seeping through her tunic, her skin, and into her.

Mahlah's answer was to reach for No'ah's hand and weave their fingers together. It felt better than a fist—better enough that she reached with her other hand for Milcah's while Mahlah did the same with Hoglah, and Hoglah with Tirzah.

Together. Sisters. Just like before.

But this was nothing like before. This time, their elders were arrayed behind them, not before or at their side. It should have felt supportive, like when Abba had stood behind them, teaching them to nock an arrow and watching to see how straight it flew. Or like when Imma would steady a little one on her feet and then let go, standing behind her to see if she wobbled and folded or took that first step forward on her own.

It didn't feel like either of those. It felt, instead, like they were shoving the Daughters forward as unwilling sacrifices and then scooting back out of the way of God's wrath.

Why should God be wrathful though? They'd done nothing wrong. He had given them His favor weeks ago. Why would He rescind it now?

This time, Moses had been made aware of the request before they came, hence the summons. He wasn't even in his judgment seat when they filed in, so they were arrayed here in front of an empty chair. No'ah's stomach curled into a knot inside her, growing tighter and smaller with every second that passed.

The only time in her life she'd seen their leader up close was a month ago, when he'd given his first edict for them. She'd only ever seen him smiling, contemplative. Never angry or stern—though stories were still told about the times when he lashed out against the children of Israel, making them drink the dust of their golden idols and raining condemnation upon them for their faithlessness as he struck a rock to call forth water. Simon had even been near enough to see him smash the original Tablets, on which God Himself had written the Ten Words—he'd only been a lad then, of course. But he told the tale with a memory clear as water.

A kind and thoughtful Moses had been terrifying enough. She didn't know what she'd do if he came out stern and foreboding.

The curtain rustled, and their leader stepped out, Joshua following close on his heels. No'ah's pent up breath leaked out.

He didn't look angry or fearsome, anyway. That was surely good. He just looked…concerned. Thoughtful, but not in quite the same way he had before. He took his seat a little more slowly than the month before, moved his gaze along the line of them with slow consideration.

Did he know? Did he know that Mahlah wanted to marry outside the clan, and that was why this complaint had come before him? Or had it been presented as a hypothetical situation?

He smiled, but it looked to No'ah as though there was a note of sorrow in it. Or perhaps that sorrow was just in her own eyes, and she'd see it reflected wherever she looked. She gave Mahlah's fingers a squeeze.

Moses cleared his throat. "Thank you for coming again. The elders of the tribe of Manasseh have brought a question to my attention. It has arisen based on my previous ruling on the matter of the daughters of Zelophehad inheriting their father's portion in the Promised Land in absence of any sons. Their concern is that if the daughters marry outside their tribe, then it will amount to the tribe of their husbands taking land that belongs by rights to Manasseh."

He paused, his gaze moving over their line once more, and then beyond them, to the men gathered. The elders, yes, but there were many more back there than them. There were Cozbi and Danijel and all the others who had gone to Simon's with him. There were Asher and Micah and Eldad and Chanoch. Abiram and Izik and Kapriel and Uriel and Seth. Anyone with an interest in the outcome—meaning anyone who had been either pursuing one of them or counted them as a friend or cousin.

Moses drew in a long breath. "This is a situation the Hebrews have never encountered—we have always been a wandering people. Even when we consider Abraham and Isaac and Jacob himself, inheriting land was never a question to be considered. How to ensure fairness among the brethren is a more complicated matter than I had realized. But I took the question to the Lord, and He has advised me, as I trusted He would."

He paused, pursed his lips, and settled his gaze on Mahlah. No'ah squeezed her fingers even more tightly. "The Lord wants the best for His people," Moses said softly. "All of them, but also each of them, individually. It is why He has given us a Law to govern not only our outward actions but our innermost hearts."

Mahlah shifted her weight from one foot to the other. No'ah bit her lip until it ached.

Moses continued, widening his gaze again. "The Lord has said that the daughters of Zelophehad should marry whom they think best, but they must marry within their father's tribe.

This is the only way to ensure that each tribe's portion remains with that tribe. So it shall be for any daughter who inherits from her father."

Other voices sprang up like a fount, the words gushing over No'ah without any comprehension. She heard the victory in some of the tones, the resignation in others, the compassion in a few. She heard Eldad's sigh—he was of the tribe of Judah—and Uriel's sharp intake of breath.

But mostly she heard the way Mahlah fought not to react at all. She felt her sister's fingers go limp within her own but saw how her shoulders refused to slump. She caught a whiff of honey and cinnamon as her sister shifted, tasted betrayal on her own tongue.

How could God do this to Mahlah? How could He have taken away the one choice she'd ever considered making for herself? Had she not served their family faithfully all her life? Had she not served the Lord even more faithfully, even in the face of losing both their parents? Why? Why had He done this to her?

Mahlah's struggle sounded like even breathing, each breath in and out so measured that No'ah found herself counting *one-two-three-four, one-two-three-four* along with her. It sounded like heavy silence. It sounded like delicate pottery shattering but still holding its form, crackling and popping and just waiting for the chance to fall to pieces.

She wouldn't, not here. Not anywhere with others' eyes and ears. Possibly not even before the younger girls. She would smile and assure them that God was just and merciful. She would set a good example for Tirzah, who had just lost one of her favorite suitors as well. She would do what had to be done, because that was Mahlah, had always been Mahlah, and she wouldn't even rant or rail over it, because she never did. Didn't even know how.

But No'ah knew. No'ah would do it for her, internally if not aloud, not yet. If Mahlah wouldn't let herself be angry with God and Moses, No'ah would do it on her behalf, and it began now with more silent cries. *Why, God? Why do You treat Your daughter this way?*

Only when Milcah rubbed a hand over No'ah's arm did she realize she was trembling.

Mahlah let go of her hand and stepped forward, head inclined in respect. "Thank you, my lord, for going before the Lord again on our behalf. We are honored by His attention and appreciate your time."

No'ah had to bite her lip to keep from contradicting her sister. Her fingers curled into her palm again, on the hand that Mahlah had dropped. *She* wasn't honored, wasn't grateful. She was mad as a nest of hornets.

At Moses's nod, Mahlah turned around, making a little shooing motion with her hands that was all the permission No'ah needed. She spun on her heel, letting go of Milcah's hand, and charged for the door. It meant elbowing her way through some of the gloating tribesmen, but that didn't bother her at all.

She needed fresh air, sunshine, and preferably some wide-open space to run through.

Cozbi blocked her path, and the smirk he gave her made her lift her fist lift a few inches. "Why are you so angry, No'ah? Did you have a suitor from another tribe too? Or—no, of course not. No one's lining up to fight for *you*, are they?"

Abiram stepped between them, his back to No'ah as he faced Cozbi but the tension obvious in his shoulders. "Speak to her that way again, Cozbi, and it will be *you* before the elders for your bad behavior. I won't have it."

If it were Mahlah, she would have said something soothing to their guardian, assuring him she wasn't offended. If it were Hoglah, she'd dance her way past him, showing his words meant nothing to her. If it were Milcah, she'd lift her chin and glide by like a queen. If it were Tirzah, she'd laugh it off.

She wasn't any of her sisters, though. She was her, and she probably would have done something stupid and hot-headed, had Izik's arm not come around her waist and steered her quickly out the door.

"Easy, Hornet," he murmured.

And just like that, some of the anger blew away in the breeze and a breath of laughter slipped out of her lips. The knots in her shoulders unraveled as the afternoon sunshine poured over her. "How do you always know what I'm thinking?"

"Many years of long practice. Come on—you need to get away from people for a while."

Rather than lead her all the way through the camp and out into the familiar stretch of land beyond their own tents, he took her straight through the heart of Issachar and out into the wilderness as opposite their own as one could get.

She'd crossed this land before, as they set up camp in this location. But it looked altogether different without all the people and livestock tromping across it, and she hadn't been back around to this side of camp since then. The air was just as refreshing, but the landscape, new to her eyes, was far more interesting than the familiar trees and streams and boulders.

Izik led her through it with what looked like ease—either he'd been over here before or he didn't mind not knowing precisely where they were going. They stayed within view of the tents at all times, slowly walking the perimeter of camp, which would lead them, eventually, home.

She was in no rush, either, to get there or to talk about all the things churning angrily inside. Izik, being Izik, didn't push for conversation. He just walked—until he paused, squinting at something caught between a few rocks.

No'ah followed his gaze, frowning at the colorful feathers. Not that it was odd to find feathers lying about—but there were several of them, the colors varied and exotic and bright, and arranged almost like... "An arrow?"

"Looks like it." Izik crouched down and tugged until the shaft of the arrow pulled free from the space between the rocks. He ran his fingers over the arrowhead, along the shaft, up to the feathers. "I've never seen a fletching like this."

Neither had she. There was some variety among the People, of course, depending on each one's preferences, but she'd only ever seen three or four. This one had a double row of three, and a feather trailing off the back too, almost as if it were decorative. "A child playing with a new design?"

"Possible, I suppose. Or." He looked up, away from camp. Toward Shittim, where it nestled just beyond the horizon.

The sun was hot, the wind warm, but a shiver overtook her. She knew, of course, that the Moabites came to the camp. They traded here, just as Israelites traveled to the city. Most of them were peaceful. Quite likely, if one had shot an arrow this close to the camp, it was to ward off a predator at dusk.

But then there was the truth she'd done a good job of not thinking about until now: one or some of them had killed Abba. It had been a dagger of Moabite design in his back, and while that didn't guarantee who did it—an Israelite could have purchased the weapon from them—it was the most likely answer. No Israelite had such a grudge against her father that he'd stab him in the back.

She knew that the elders had investigated, just to be certain. There had been footsteps in the dirt leading away from the boulder and then hoofprints at the next rock, heading back toward the city. They'd come to the conclusion that it must have been a crime of opportunity, conjecturing that they'd intended to rob him, but they'd heard the group of young people coming and had run away before they'd been able to unloop the goods from his back.

Worrying over it and yearning for justice had been two instincts she'd deliberately set aside, given the new concern of her sisters' marriages. They were two instincts that had seemed impossible to satisfy anyway—of course there were raiders and robbers and thieves and murderers hiding in the wilderness. There always were. They always avoided the camp as a whole, but from time to time, individuals caught away from their brethren became victims of violence and greed. Such was the life of nomads. Such was life everywhere, she suspected. She hated it, but she had no hope of changing it.

Finding justice for her father would have been possible and sought, had the footsteps led back into camp. Had an Israelite murdered him, the culprit would have been rooted out and punished—blood for blood, life for life. But a Moabite who had fled to Shittim for sanctuary? Her elders could demand the murderer be turned over, but the city's king was unlikely to comply. Why should he turn his city upside down looking for one thief who'd taken the life of one stranger? More likely, he'd see that a mighty warrior had been taken out and consider it a favor. No matter how open the trading had been with Shittim or any other city, the kings of the various city-states never considered them allies. Only enemies.

Such was the reasoning that had allowed her to shove those instincts aside. But they reared again now, seeing that foreign arrow so near to Israel's camp. What if it hadn't been just one person who saw a dreadful opportunity and had taken it? Or what if that person had come back, looking for his next victim?

Her arms folded over her middle, a stance not of stubbornness but of a need for comfort no human could give. "I don't like it."

Izik stood again, slipping the arrow into his bag, his gaze still trained on the distance. "That makes two of us. Come on—let's get home. I want to show Abba. They should all be back by the time we get there."

No'ah fell in beside him without complaint, matching her pace to his without trouble. She didn't want to think about enemies being so close. She didn't want to think about the fact that her sister's hopes for love had just been ripped from her. She didn't want to think about the way her heart ached anytime she was still for a few seconds together. Missing Abba. Missing the ease of the life they used to have. Missing the days when they were just them, not the Five Daughters.

So she thought about the least worrisome of any of her options—Cozbi's insults. "I'm not as distasteful as Cozbi says, am I?"

Izik slanted a look at her, like she was a fool for asking.

Maybe she was. She shrugged. "I don't care what *he* thinks—but I'll need to marry someone eventually. What if this fellow you've picked out for me doesn't like me?"

Was that a roll of Izik's eyes? He was facing forward again, so she couldn't be sure. Until he snorted, which pretty much confirmed the suspicion. "He likes you. And you like him."

Like—that meant she knew him already. And got along with him. Which ruled out Cozbi but very few others, honestly. She knew half the young men in the tribe and quite a few from others. "He's—but wait. Is he of our tribe?"

"Yes, No'ah." He glanced over at her again, that mix of amusement and incredulity on his lips that he gave her so often in place of a normal smile. "Are you really just going to take my advice and marry whoever I say you should?"

She shrugged again. "Seems like a better option than agonizing over my own decision and second-guessing whichever one I make. You have good taste—and you know me better than anyone but my sisters. If anyone has a hope of choosing the right husband for me, it's you."

CHAPTER ELEVEN

Night crept in from the east while the last pastels still clung to the horizon in the west, a whisper of beauty and promise of peace. *Night may come*, those colors said, *but hope isn't lost. Darkness always gives way again to light.*

Mahlah sat a stone's throw from her tent, willing herself to believe that promise. To cling to what her heart didn't feel just now. To believe what felt like empty promises. Over and again she repeated silently the words Moses had spoken—that God wanted not only *their* best, but *her* best. That He created laws not just for everyone but for each one. That she wasn't just an example. She was an individual, and He knew what she needed too. That even while limiting her choices, He's still left the choice in her hands. *Let them marry whom they think best.*

She knew the words. They just didn't mean anything right now.

Kapriel and Izik were outside their own tent two down from hers. Not close enough to listen to anything she chose to say, but close enough to see if anyone approached her. Close enough to hear it if she screamed. Their presence was both comfortable and invisible, easy to dismiss from her awareness as quickly as she thought of it.

It was their stirring, though, their standing that made her aware of the sound of footsteps approaching from the south. She spotted the approaching figure before she could make out in the quickly falling night who it was, but something about the way he raised his hand in greeting made her both relax and come to alertness.

Kapriel and Izik both sat back down, and Uriel soon slid up beside her and took a seat on the ground a few inches away. "Sorry I couldn't come sooner," he said, voice low enough that it likely wouldn't travel through the thick walls of the tent and definitely not all the way to their neighbors. "I thought it best to wait when I saw the crowd here."

Mahlah nodded. All the elders of the tribe had been here all evening, lecturing them as if the word of Moses—the very word of God—hadn't been instruction enough. They'd gone so far as to recite a list of every unmarried man over the age of twenty in Manasseh, and the family he came from. It had not only taken forever, it had been unnecessary. They'd already made their own lists. They knew all the information given.

With every recitation, her throat had gone a little tighter with guilt and dread. *She* was the reason for all this. Not her sisters, not some abstract question—her. Her decisions, her choices, her preferences. Her heart's yearning, which Abba had always encouraged her to explore, had landed them back before Moses and led to an edict straight from God, contradicting all she wanted.

Mostly, her sisters had been cheerful enough about it all. Hoglah and Asher had in fact approached Abiram and asked if a betrothal contract could be drawn up as soon as possible. Micah had stood with Milcah away from the crowd and whispered something to her that made a beautiful, secret smile bloom on her lips—Mahlah suspected another betrothal agreement would be requested in the next day or two too.

Tirzah had merely shrugged and said, happy as though it were a bit of a relief, "I suppose that narrows down my choices for me. Chanoch *does* make me laugh like no one else...."

Only No'ah had been silent and stony, and Mahlah knew it wasn't because of any anger on her own part—it was on Mahlah's behalf. No'ah hadn't set her sights on *anyone*, so she wasn't angry about having her own choices taken away, unless the principle of it offended her. But no, No'ah wasn't the sort to get upset over hypotheticals. She was the sort to get upset when someone hurt her sister.

Mahlah appreciated that, on the one hand. On the other, it just added another level of guilt. Because No'ah wasn't just angry at Cozbi for raising the question—she was angry at the Lord for giving the answer she didn't want. And the last thing Mahlah wanted was to be the reason her sister lost even a grain of faith.

Uriel said nothing more for a moment, just sat still as a rock. Perhaps he was waiting for Mahlah to speak first, but what could she say? Words, introduction, possibilities had swirled through her mind all afternoon and evening, but none of them had seemed right.

Eventually, he let out a long breath. "Mahlah...this doesn't change my feelings for you. It doesn't change that I want to marry you. If that means you come to me without a son's inheritance—why should I care about that? I wanted this before such things were even a possibility. I want it still now."

She turned to look at him, though there was scant light with which to do so, and she found herself frustrated with the darkness. She wanted to see his face. His eyes. "I…" But she didn't know how to respond. Was that even an option? Moses hadn't given a condition of what would happen if an inheriting daughter chose *not* to marry within her tribe—it hadn't been presented as a possibility. Could she…could she simply forfeit the inheritance? Trade her father's legacy for the marriage she wanted?

"I don't care if you don't have your own portion in the Promised Land." A strange *something* entered his voice— something she'd never heard before. Something dark—no, bright. Bright with resentment, like a coal smoldering in the grass. "Honestly, I'm not sure I care about *my* portion of the Promised Land. What if I don't want to be tied to one place, allotted to me by Moses or Joshua or whoever among the elders is given the task? What if I want to wander, like our people have always done? Become a trader or a scout or a merchant? What if I want to stay *here* instead of crossing over the Jordan?"

"Here?" Why would he want to remain in a land where they were strangers—and apart from all their families?

"Why not? It's a beautiful land, and Shittim is a good city. I can imagine making a home there."

"You…" Life in a city? One with walls and gates and… She shook her head. They would have cities of their own in the Promised Land. She knew that. Many Israelites would end up living in them—some they would build with their own hands, others they would take from the heathen the Lord had promised to clear out for them. She'd just never imagined *herself* in one of those cities. She'd imagined instead a home nestled in the hills, with water flowing freely nearby. She imagined a husband planting crops and tending vines and learning how to turn the grapes into wine. She imagined her children running free with their cousins.

"Or if that's not what you want, then we can cross the Jordan with the others—live on my portion in Benjamin. If that would make you happy."

Would it? Of course that was the logical thing, what wives always did—they went to their husband's home, their husband's family. She knew that. She just hadn't yet considered that marrying him, giving up *her* inheritance, would also mean giving up her sisters.

There would be far more than an encampment between them once they took the Land. She'd not be able to walk to them and home again in an afternoon. They would be miles apart—days, perhaps weeks of travel. Her breath leaked from her, slow and thoughtful.

Did she love him enough to give up everything for him? It seemed that half of her cried out *Yes!* But the other half wasn't as certain. There were so many consequences to whatever decision she made. So much at stake. "I don't know what would make me happy," she admitted in a whisper.

"Because you've spent all your life concerned only with what will make your sisters happy. That's to your credit—but you deserve happiness too, Mahlah. And I would give it to you. In whatever form you want."

"I know you would." Or he'd try, anyway. But what if true happiness couldn't be given by any man? That had always been her uncles' arguments against them choosing their own husbands—that happiness wasn't about the feelings with which you began a relationship. It was about the choices made together every day of your lives. If she married him, she'd have to choose for it to be enough. To find her happiness in him, not in her sisters. To build a life wherever he wanted, not among her own tribe.

Things she would have agreed to in a heartbeat before the summons from Moses. But somehow, hearing him say that the Lord had commanded her to marry someone from Manasseh...she didn't know how to disobey that.

Perhaps Uriel heard all the things she didn't say. His breath whooshed out, and he shoved agitated fingers into his hair. "I cannot understand why the Lord is so cruel."

"He isn't!" The words flew from her lips without pausing for any input from her mind—because that was one thing her heart had never questioned. Goodness was defined by God. How could He be anything but? "He is the giver of every blessing."

"And the taker of it too. He took your mother, your father. My father. My mother gave up everything to serve Him, and she's led a life of misery, feeling always the outcast among the people she chose as her own. And now this—I finally find you, and God takes you away."

What the Lord gives is His to take, Abba had always said. *Blessed be the name of the Lord.* Her lips parted, ready to echo the words, but something stayed her. Perhaps it was the set of his jaw, caught in the last vestiges of daylight.

She reached over instead and rested her fingers on the wrist he had propped on his drawn-up knees. "I don't know what the future will bring, Uriel. But I know it will be good, because that's what He promises those who are faithful to Him."

Uriel didn't look over at her through the darkness. In fact, he turned his face away. She could practically feel his pain and anger pulsing through his veins. Like No'ah's, in a way, but not. No'ah's anger was purely sympathetic—Uriel's was very personal.

She knew so little about him, in some ways. What had he thought of the father his mother had such mixed thoughts about? What hurt and pain had he suffered in his childhood because of who his mother was? Were those things part of why he could now question God's goodness and mercy? She wished she knew, wanted to know...but didn't. And wasn't sure she'd ever have the chance to.

She squeezed his wrist.

He covered her fingers with his, lifted them, and brought them to his mouth. The kiss he pressed to her knuckles made her heart gallop as much as one to her lips would have done. Perhaps. "*You* are the best thing I've ever found in my life," he whispered against her hand. "If He takes you from me..."

Another weight banded around her chest. She couldn't resent him for it, no more than she could resent her little sisters for relying on her when they were children or Abba for clinging to his love of her mother. It was simply the cost of caring. Of living. Of building a family.

Even so, it made breathing more difficult. As for words— she had none.

He didn't wait for any. He leaned over, pressed his lips lightly to hers—lightly, but lingering. Then, after an eternal heartbeat, he pulled away, released her fingers, and stood. "Whatever you decide."

With that he turned and melted back into the deepening night.

Mahlah fought air into her lungs, back out. In and out again. She didn't know if she wanted to press her fingertips to her lips in rapture or sob until every last drop of emotion was spent.

What a strange, horrible, beautiful day. From the sun rising over the boulder at which her father had died, to Cozbi's violence, to meeting Uriel's mother…from another audience with Moses to this moment that was part loss and part promise.

She didn't know what to do. Every decision looked wrong.

Kap settled beside her, on the side opposite where Uriel had been. His presence didn't startle, no more than it could soothe. Nothing could.

Even so, she rested her head against his shoulder when he scooted near enough for her to do so. "Tell me what to do." Words she'd never spoken before, certainly not to the boy she'd laughed and fought with all through her childhood.

Kapriel breathed a laugh that was more sorrow than mirth. "Would that I could, Mahl. But this is your choice—no one else's."

"Is it?" She squeezed her eyes shut, which only served to show her how dark the night had grown—she scarcely noticed the difference. "Moses didn't present it as a choice. He didn't say what the consequences would be if I *didn't* marry a clansman."

"He didn't. But that's no reason the choice isn't there. You could give up the inheritance. Follow your heart."

But it wasn't about the inheritance, not in the physical sense. It was about her father's legacy—that's all it had *ever* been about. Honoring him. Allowing him to live on, as he so deserved. "Moses rewrote every tradition of our people when he gave us the right to be treated like sons. How can I dishonor both him and Abba by tossing that aside? And yet Abba's wish for us wasn't land or possessions—it was a marriage of love, like what he and Imma shared."

"It's a hard choice." Kapriel rested his head on hers. "You're not going to sucker me into making it for you either."

"Some friend you are." But joking about it, even for just a few seconds, helped.

"Iz probably would, if you asked him. He's claiming to have single-handedly steered the other girls toward their perfect husbands."

A snort of laughter snuck out. "Even No'ah?"

"Hmm. He's mum on who it is but says he has hers sorted out too."

"Interesting. Perhaps I *will* ask him what I should do. He's clearly a miracle worker—not on the scale of Moses, perhaps, but…"

She wouldn't. They both knew that. She had been given the gift of choice by her father, by her uncles, by God Himself. She had been presented with the opportunity to be counted with the sons of Manasseh by Moses. Whatever she decided, it would be her decision.

Kapriel sighed. "I never would have guessed when I introduced Uriel to everyone that this was what would happen. I like him. He's become a friend, but…I admit it, Mahl. I don't know why he's captured your heart so fully, so quickly."

"Because no girl has ever captured yours. It makes no sense, but once you've experienced it, you'll understand."

He grunted his opinion of that. "I'm just as happy not understanding. We have many battles ahead of us. I want to fight for our people, unhindered. I certainly don't want to make anyone mourn for me if I fall."

"We'd all mourn!"

"Not like a wife would."

"True." She scanned the sky, looking for the first shards of light to glitter their way into the heavens, but none were visible yet. At least not in front of her. "Maybe that's what I should do too," she said, making sure her voice gave away the joke. "Postpone all marriage decisions until after we've settled in the land and fight alongside you—if I'm being treated like a son, I mean."

Kapriel chuckled. "It could work. You're tall as most of the men—if we put some armor on you to hide your figure, no one would be the wiser. And we all know you can outshoot us with a bow."

"I could use some more training with swords and spears though." She smiled, just because it was nice to talk about something ridiculous even for a minute.

"With the Lord fighting on our side? He could strengthen your arm and make your aim true for you. You'd be fine."

"True. I'll see you on the battlefield, then."

"I'll save you a place at my side." He lifted his head, dropped a brotherly kiss onto the top of hers, and straightened.

Mahlah did too. "Thanks, Kap." He hadn't exactly given her clarity, and he certainly hadn't offered any advice. But he'd reminded her of who she was—Zelophehad's eldest daughter.

CHAPTER TWELVE

No'ah didn't care much for sheep, it was true, but trailing Izik to his father's fold had proven to be a good way to escape the pressure inside her own tent, so there she was, perched on one of the piles of rocks that marked the border of Manasseh pasture, watching as Iz and Kap herded the animals into the pen they'd built months ago.

One of the lambs darted away from the rest of the flock, bleating in fear and running out toward the open spaces instead of back to the safety of the fold. Kapriel's attention didn't stray from his task with the other sheep, but Izik tossed his hands up in a gesture of helpless frustration.

No'ah laughed and jumped down from her perch, moving the same direction as the lamb. "I'll get her!" She didn't have Hoglah's way with the creatures, but she'd still had to chase after her fair share of runaway lambs over the years.

This one was quicker than she'd anticipated. She only wanted to get close enough to call to it in the singsong her middle sister always used, but the silly thing kept running faster whenever she drew near enough to try the trick.

She tried it anyway, hearing Hoglah in her head, warning her that chasing a lamb only scared it more. She stood still, crouched down, sang the song Hoglah always sang.

The lamb veered in a new direction, but it wasn't back toward her. "Stupid animals," No'ah muttered, pushing back to her feet. She looked behind her, rolling her eyes at how far from the fold they'd already gone.

At least the creature wasn't headed toward open wilderness now, just along the lines of livestock that ringed the camp. Which meant she wouldn't be out of sight of all the many Israelites caring for their herds. Even so, she somehow wasn't surprised when she spotted Izik jogging after her. He'd taken his orders for her and her sisters to never be without a guardian seriously and was always tagging after one or another of them when they did something as mundane as go to fetch water from the river.

Maybe he'd have better luck calling to the lamb. She tried again, but the animal kept trotting south. "You try," she said by way of greeting when he reached her.

He did—to no greater success. They ended up trailing the little ewe until she grew tired, by which time they were well beyond the flocks of Manasseh. When he scooped up the runaway at long last, No'ah heaved a sigh. "Looks as if we have a bit of a hike back."

Izik slung the lamb around his neck, anchoring it there with hands on front and back legs, and grinned. "And a fine day it is for a walk."

She flicked a smile at him, though it fell all the way into a frown when movement beyond him caught her eye. "Is that Uriel?"

She hadn't seen much of him the last two days, since Moses's new edict. She knew he'd come to talk with Mahlah that first evening and suspected he kept his distance now simply to give her sister time to make her choice. And because the whole tribe seemed bent on keeping any outsiders far from their tent.

It must be killing him, if he loved her the way he said he did.

Izik spun, nodding. "Looks like it. Did you want to catch up with him?"

Did she? It felt odd to, on one hand, without Mahlah there. She'd never actually had a conversation with him other than with her sister. But then, shouldn't she? She wanted to gauge for herself if his love was as true as he claimed. If he was worth the possibility of her sister giving up her legacy for a future with him. No'ah nodded. "Let's."

Catching up to Uriel proved as challenging as chasing after the lamb had been. They tried calling to him, but the wind snatched their voices away—either that, or he was deliberately ignoring them. She doubted that, though. He never even looked over his shoulder, just followed a trickling stream up the hill, through a grove of trees.

She'd never been this direction before, to know where he might be going. "Does he have his bow? Is he hunting?"

"I didn't see one—though if he's after small game, he could have his slingshot. He's good with it."

It seemed just as likely that he was seeking quiet and solitude, in which case he probably wouldn't appreciate their interruption. She slowed, dragging in a long breath. "Maybe we should turn back."

"Soon," Izik agreed, the light in his eyes one of curiosity. "I've never followed this path. I want to see where it goes."

Her lips twitched. Curiosity over the terrain more than his friend, it seemed. "I won't argue, if Little Lamb doesn't."

Little Lamb seemed perfectly content around his shoulders, her head resting between her legs. She must have truly worn herself out. Izik reached to rub a finger over her nose and kept moving.

It was a pretty spot—she could see why Uriel retreated here. After they crested the hill, the sounds of animals and the busy camp fell away, filling her ears instead with the trill of birds, the gurgle of the stream, and the song of the wind through the tall boughs of the trees. No'ah pulled in a long, contented breath that smelled of grass and flowers and fresh water and something else, something smoky and sweet.

Izik came to a halt so abruptly she almost ran into his back. Then he backed up a step, nearly stepping on her toes.

Ordinarily, she would have snapped out a half-laughed warning, but something about the hush of this glen made her simply move aside instead. And look to see what he'd seen.

She wished she hadn't. Uriel had crossed the stream, climbed up onto a rock, and was kneeling before…something. She couldn't tell from here what it was, exactly, only that it was wooden.

Incense, that was the smoky-sweet smell. He'd lit a cone of it before the wooden thing and bowed low, until his head touched the rock.

No'ah stumbled backward, horror blooming in her chest. An idol. Uriel, the man who claimed to love her sister, was worshiping an *idol*.

Her stomach churning, she spun around just as Izik did, racing back down the hillside and out of sight. The moss and grasses padded their retreating steps as they had done their approaching ones, for which she was glad.

She didn't want Uriel spotting them and running after them. She didn't want him to offer any excuses. She didn't want to look in his eyes and see the man Mahlah loved and have to try to reconcile him with *this*.

By the time they reached the bottom of the hill again, she heaved to a stop, let her knees fold, let herself sink down into the grass and wildflowers, let her eyes slide closed. She wasn't ready to face the rest of Israel yet either.

"How?" It emerged more as a quaver than a question. "How could he do this? Doesn't he know that the Lord is purging the unfaithful from the camp? How could he worship an idol made by man and yet claim to love Mahlah, who loves the Lord above all?"

Izik sank to the ground beside her. The weight of his hand settled on her head. "I don't know. I don't—I never suspected." His voice sounded cracked and broken, just like she felt. And she wasn't even the one in love with him. How would Mahlah feel, when she learned this?

No'ah squeezed her eyes shut tight. "Was it a ba'al? I don't honestly know what they look like."

"Maybe? I've never seen one with my own eyes either." His hand stroked over her hair—she imagined him doing the same thing with his other hand to the lamb. Calming them both, and himself in the process. "This will be worse for her than if we saw him with another woman."

"So much worse." Infidelity to her, when they weren't even officially betrothed, would have stung but left her whole. Infidelity to the Lord would crush her, because it wasn't just her dreams that were lost—it was *him*. "Poor Mahlah."

She wished she didn't have to tell her. Hoped that, when she returned to the tent, her sister would simply announce that she'd made her decision and would marry within the tribe. Then there'd be no need to destroy her image of the man who'd captured her heart.

It wouldn't happen that way, though. She knew it wouldn't. Nothing in life ever gave her such an easy way out. Her stomach churned. "I'm going to be sick."

"No you're not. You're going to be strong. Because your sister needs you to be."

Why did he always have to be right? "I'll be strong after I'm sick."

"No'ah." Somehow, the way he said her name with half a laugh was so very normal that the urge to vomit receded, and she could sit up again. Could look at him. His gaze was bright and unflinching and *Izik*. "Let's find Kapriel first. He was the one to introduce them. He'll feel responsible for this."

She winced, but she nodded. Both of their siblings were about to have a very bad day. Worse even than her own.

They stood up and began the trek back toward camp. They'd walked several minutes in silence before Izik spoke. "It's odd, isn't it? People all over the world do that—bend the knee to their own creations and call them gods. To the people in

Shittim, it's nothing. It's normal. It's *good*. But we see it and are horrified."

"Because we know what true worship is. Because we serve a living God, not a lifeless lump of wood or clay." The words could have been Abba's—but they were her own. And speaking them didn't exactly erase the anger she felt at the Lord, but it made it…understandable.

God wasn't a person exactly, not like Iz or Mahlah. But He was alive. He was the pillar of fire and the unending cloud, He was the voice that spoke the Law into their hearts and the eyes that saw each of them, wherever they were.

She had to swallow past a lump in her throat. He saw Uriel too, there on that hilltop, worshiping something other than Him. What were the chances that He'd let that go unanswered, when they were so close to claiming His promise?

"Uriel should know that too. He's dwelt in the shadow of the cloud. He's followed the pillar of fire. He's eaten manna every day of his life. How could he turn away?"

She could only shake her head at Izik's question. She didn't understand how *any* Israelite could turn away, when they lived the miraculous. But they'd been doing it since the moment they left Israel, some of them. Perhaps for some, the miraculous became mundane. Perhaps others thought God a tyrant for imposing a Law they didn't want to keep. Perhaps…
"I don't know."

They looked for Kapriel at the sheepfold when they returned the ewe, but the cousins still there said he'd gone back into camp. They checked his family's tent, but their mother reported that he'd gone to check on Mahlah.

No'ah and Izik exchanged a glance as they stepped back into the sunshine. "Well," she said, "at least that means we only have to say it once."

Izik winced. "I'd rather not say it at all. Is it too much to ask that we walk in there and Mahlah tells us she's decided to marry within the tribe?"

She laughed, solely because of the echo of her own thoughts. "We can hope."

At the least, she hoped that they'd find Kap and Mahlah away from the others, somewhere they couldn't be overheard. But even that hope proved futile. Abiram and Keturah were there, their children with them, her own sisters there too, apart from Tirzah. Her fingers knotted in her tunic. The words didn't want to come at all—how was she to say them with *everyone* there?

"Kap, Mahlah—do you have a minute?" Izik, as usual, solved her dilemma even as she framed it, his voice sounding casual as he waved them out the door.

They both put down what they were doing—Kap was showing one of their cousins how to do something with a knife and a block of wood, Mahlah had been sewing what would become Hoglah's wedding garment—and followed them outside without a qualm.

Of course *they* had no qualms. They didn't know what was coming. But No'ah felt as though, with each step, she might buzz to pieces.

Izik led them out into the field a ways, to where they'd sat as a tribe two months ago and told stories about Abba. If only those were the sort of story she had to tell today.

When they turned to face Kapriel and Mahlah again, No'ah opened her mouth, knowing this was hers to say. It was her sister. Her sister's future. Her eyes that had first spotted Uriel, her decision to follow him. So why wouldn't the words come?

Izik shifted closer to her, so that the backs of their hands brushed where they hung. "We saw Uriel today, when we were chasing a lost lamb." He said it so simply. So easily. His voice was steady and even, though she could hear the strain in it, and no doubt they could too. "We followed him, thinking to see how he's doing. But we...we saw him..."

Funny how the cracking of Izik's voice gave her back her own. She moved her hand an inch, so that they were palm to palm. So that she could weave their fingers together. "He had a ba'al—or some sort of idol, anyway. He'd lit incense before it and was bowing to it."

She expected an explosion. A quick *"What?"* that led to demands for more explanation. She expected weeping—and perhaps a bit of teeth-gnashing for good measure.

Mahlah rather looked as though she might faint, swaying where she stood, eyes going unfocused. Kapriel reached to steady her with a hand on her arm, blinking and staring at his brother as if waiting for him to contradict No'ah.

Izik dipped his head. "I'm sorry. Both of you. We didn't confront him, we...we just ran back here."

"Maybe...you're mistaken." The words emerged choked from Kapriel's mouth, his tight expression saying he didn't believe it even as he suggested it.

No'ah shook her head. "We smelled the incense. Saw it burning. Saw the...the *thing* in front of him. He was bowing down before it."

Mahlah's eyes were still locked on nothing. "He said the Lord was cruel."

"What?" Now Kapriel asked the expected thing but with no outrage. No burst of denial. Just a dazed sort of resignation.

Mahlah's eyes slid closed, and she swayed again. No'ah dropped Izik's hand so she could move to her sister's side and slip an arm around her waist. "The other night. He said the Lord was cruel, that He'd taken everything from him. He sounded...unbelieving. But I thought it was doubt. Not this." Her eyes flew open again, and her fingers flew to her lips. "His poor mother! She'll be heartbroken."

And that was Mahlah, her concern needing someone else to rest on, other than herself. No'ah didn't know whether to hug her or shake her.

She hugged her.

Kapriel frowned. "Are you certain about that? Or is she the one who taught him to chase after other gods?"

"I'm certain. It was his father who was never committed to the Lord. She said—"

"*She* said—but he can't, because he's gone. What makes you so sure you can trust her word?"

Mahlah turned in No'ah arms. "I met her, we spoke about this very thing. I would have known if she were lying."

"Would you? Because you couldn't tell that Uriel—"

"Um." Izik stepped between Kapriel and Mahlah, hands lifted, eyes jumping from one of them to the other. "Do you really want to argue about this?"

Both sets of shoulders sagged. Kapriel rubbed a hand over his face. "Sorry, Mahl. I'm angry at *myself* for not seeing it, not you. I want someone to blame, and I'd rather it be someone still here, that I can point a finger at. Someone...someone who was at least born not one of us. Then it means the fault isn't with our own."

But it was, regardless. It was with Uriel.

Mahlah sighed. "This isn't going to get any better with time. I need to talk to him." She stepped away from No'ah, toward that path that led around the perimeter of the camp, southward toward Benjamin.

Kapriel moved to her side. "I'll go with you."

No'ah looked to Izik. Should they offer to go too? To be the eyewitnesses? But he shook his head, and she sagged in relief. If Kapriel hadn't volunteered, she would have gone, so that Mahlah wasn't alone. But she wasn't ready to see Uriel again.

She wasn't sure she ever would be.

CHAPTER THIRTEEN

Mahlah wasn't sorry when Kapriel touched her elbow and then pointed out to the countryside as they neared the tents of Benjamin. Her gaze followed where he indicated and saw the figure she'd come to recognize so easily, the one that always made her heart thrill when she spotted him.

Now, as they moved to intercept Uriel, she found herself looking for bulges under his tunic. Did he have the idol on him now? Would he dare to take it into his mother's tent? Or did he hide it out there somewhere, where no one could find it? Or where, if they did, they wouldn't know to whom it belonged?

The thumping of her heart felt like dread instead of anticipation. Pain instead of pleasure.

She'd woken early that morning determined to make her decision today, and yet still so uncertain what it should be. She'd prayed that God would make her path clear. That she would know, know down to the depths of her soul, if she should marry Uriel.

This was not the form she'd expected the answer to take.

His face lit when he spotted her—that made it even worse. She knew, as she watched him jog toward them, that he hadn't been lying about his affections. That he really would either give up or accept his own inheritance, based on what she wanted him to do. She knew he loved her.

She knew, if she ended their relationship, that he would view it as the Lord taking one more thing from him. What she couldn't wrap her mind around was the fact that he believed in the God of Abraham enough to blame Him for what he'd lost—but not enough to trust Him for what he wanted. That he could think Him *a* god but serve another instead. Or in addition to. Or…whatever he was doing.

She wanted to disbelieve her sister, but she couldn't. No'ah would never lie about something like this, and even if she tried it, she'd never have been able to fake the horror underscoring her every word. She wanted to think they'd just misunderstood, as Kapriel had suggested. But what else could his actions mean?

No. It fit. It fit with his every doubt, with the anger in his tone, with his preference of Shittim to the Promised Land. It fit with every little detail that hadn't quite made sense to her, had struck her as odd. It fit with his mother's deepest fear.

Gila hadn't been the one to introduce him to other gods— she'd been the one praying for years he wouldn't follow his father to them.

Her hands started trembling as he neared, as she saw the beauty of his smile, as his dimples creased his cheeks.

She'd fallen in love with this man who loved her but not her God. She'd have been betrothed to him by now, if Moses's latest dictate hadn't given her pause. She'd learned so much about him in the last few months, but this she'd never even imagined. Never considered.

His smile didn't dim as he drew up to them and halted. Shouldn't it have? Shouldn't he have seen in her expression, in Kapriel's, that something was desperately wrong?

"What a pleasant surprise. I wasn't sure when I'd see you again, Mahlah."

The wind blew, and she caught the scent—smoke and sweet. Incense. Her voice sounded hollow to her ears when she asked, "Where have you been, Uriel?"

His smile flickered, but it didn't die, not entirely. He motioned toward the wilderness. "In my favorite glen—you remember the one I told you about, where I saw the fawn a few weeks ago?"

She remembered the story. It had brought a smile to her lips, provided an image of calm and peace she'd needed amidst all the chaos. She'd never seen the place. He said he'd show it to her someday, but the opportunity had never come.

Kapriel's jaw had a dangerous set to it, one she'd only seen a few times in life. It matched the way his hands had curled into fists. "And what were you doing there?"

If her tone was hollow, Kapriel's was boiling over. Uriel's brows didn't seem to know whether to lift in question or crash together in confusion and tried on both expressions before settling low. "I beg your pardon?"

Was it guilt in his tone? Or just bewilderment at being asked such a question?

Kap shook his head. "You were seen today, at your little secret place. With your little secret god, before whom you were bowing down."

She was watching Uriel's face carefully. For weeks, months, she'd been studying him, memorizing his every expression. She saw the flicker of panic in his eyes and then the resignation. She saw the hardness creep into each amber fleck. She saw the way his smile went cool.

"Seen by whom?"

"Reliable witnesses with nothing to gain by this revelation." Kap took a step forward, but then he paused. He let out a breath, and the fight seemed to go out with it, his shoulders sagging and fists relaxing back into fingers and palms. "Why, Uriel? Why would you do this? Why would you forsake the Almighty?"

In a different conversation, the little huff of breath Uriel released might have sounded like a laugh. In this one, it sounded like thunder in her ears. "I didn't forsake the God of Abraham—He forsook *me*. He forsook my mother, after she gave up *everything* to serve Him."

At the look Kapriel flashed her over his shoulder, Mahlah frowned. "Your mother?"

"She renounced everything to become part of Israel, and what was her reward? A husband who barely tolerated her and a lifetime of suspicion and doubt." Uriel shook his head, his own jaw now set in a fighting stance. "She should have stayed with her own people. Waited for her family. Remained loyal to Ba'al. He would have protected her. But no, she came *here*, with these people, and she's paid the price every day of her life. Your God has never shown her a *shred* of compassion— and Ba'al has punished her too, despite all the offerings her family has made on her behalf."

Mahlah didn't mean to back up a step. She'd just done it before she could even think about it. "She has no family elsewhere. She said her parents died, she had no siblings."

His gaze landed on her. "She had an uncle, cousins. Traders—they'd been away from her city when her parents died, but as soon as word reached them, they hurried back to her. But it was too late. She'd already run to the Israelites, and they'd already destroyed the city."

They. They had destroyed the city, not *we.*

Kapriel shifted. "She told you this?"

Uriel did laugh this time, a bark of it that flashed like lightning. "Imma? Of course not! She tries to pretend that old life never happened, that this is all she ever wanted, that she is a child of her precious I Am."

"Then how—"

"Our uncle and cousins told me." He was only a step away, but with those words, he seemed miles removed. "They'd followed the camp of Israel at a distance and saw her among them. They tried to make contact a few times, but she wouldn't acknowledge them. But whenever their trade routes came close, they'd come to the camp. They saw when she'd married. When she'd had me. They made friends with my father, making sure to give him the best deals on their wares. And when I was old enough, they told me who they were. How much they loved my mother, how much...how much they missed her."

Sounding as though tears clogged his voice now, Uriel lifted a fist, rested it against his heart. "Israel claims its God loves them, they claim a Law that tells them to love their neighbor, but she has never been shown anything but contempt here. Her family, though—her family has sought her, sought *me* all these years. *They* are the ones who understand love. *Their* god doesn't hover over them in a horrible cloud, demanding they do the impossible. Ba'al promises pleasure and wealth. Following him is *easy*."

"At what cost?" Kapriel's volume crept up with each word. "What does this easy way gain his followers? Abomination and sin! A race of people who kill their own children and force women into prostitution at his temples—"

"Sin defined by *your* God—"

"Yes! The Creator of the world has the *right* to tell us what is sin and what is good!"

"As if any one being could actually create everything. It's a ridiculous notion, and I—"

"Stop!" Mahlah stepped between them before their clenched-again fists could raise and try to pound their words into each other. Kapriel might have been training for battle for years, but he wasn't a fighter like this, not usually. Uriel…she didn't know. She'd never heard of him coming to blows with his friends or cousins or rivals, but he'd lived a lifetime in Benjamin before she'd met him.

What she knew was that yelling about who was right and who wrong, whether God was indeed merciful and just and all-powerful, would accomplish nothing. It wouldn't change Uriel's mind and would only harden his heart.

What she knew was that the *why* of his stance didn't change what it meant. For her. For them.

The world blurred behind her tears, his face reduced to a blend of colors, light, and darkness as she tried to look at him through them. She waited for him to focus on her instead of Kapriel. Waited for his posture to relax. Waited for him to sag.

"This matters so much to you?"

He had to ask? Her tears thickened. "This is *all* that matters. I could have given up my inheritance, Uriel. I could have given up the desire of watching my sisters' children grow up. But I can't give up my God."

"I didn't ask you to—I wouldn't."

She shook her head. "That isn't the way the Lord works. You surely know that. All His Law, all His instructions are to remind us to be pure and undefiled—to remind us that He is a jealous God and will permit no other to stand with Him, in our hearts or in our homes or in His camp."

This time he was the one to take a step back. "So you say. But my father lived decades without serving Him."

"And then he was struck down." Kapriel, voice harsh.

Only because she'd blinked the tears out onto her cheeks could she see the look Uriel sent him, at once hurt and frustrated. "Everyone dies eventually. You can't credit each death to your God striking him down. He caught a fever. He died. That's all."

"God is purging the ranks before we cross the Jordan," Kapriel insisted. "Don't cross Him, Uriel. I beg you. It won't end well. You have to know that, what with the plague—"

"Plagues strike everyone from time to time. Again, no proof of your God's power."

Had she known him at all? Mahlah felt as though her every limb had tripled in weight, dragging her down. "The miracle isn't in the coming of the plague—it's in the fact that it only struck those who had taken pagan wives."

Uriel held out his arms. "And it left me standing. So obviously your God either can't see how little I love Him, or He doesn't actually care. Either way is fine by me."

She stared at him for a long moment, letting his words rattle through her, ring in her ears, thud to a rest in her heart. Letting all the dreams of the last months wither and die before her eyes. Letting it hurt. Letting the hurt strengthen her resolve.

After an infinite moment, she turned away. "Goodbye, Uriel."

"Mahlah—wait!" He reached for her arm, his fingers gentle on it where Cozbi's had been rough only a couple of days before. "I love you. Please, don't walk away from me. If it means this much to you, I'll abandon the ba'al. I'll never burn incense to it again. I'll cut off communication with my mother's family. That's what God demands, isn't it? That we put aside the other gods. I'll do that. For you."

She went even heavier, so heavy it was a wonder the earth didn't swallow her whole as it had done to the sons of Korah. She shook her head. "No. That isn't all He asks. He asks that you *repent*. That you turn from those ways and turn *to* Him. That you believe. And you can't do that just for me."

His fingers tightened a bit on her arm—not enough to hurt, just enough to show her that he felt something more than what his face revealed. He held her gaze for a long moment.

And then he dropped his hand. "You're really walking away? Even though you love me. Though I love you. Though it'll break my mother's heart."

He dared to bring Gila into this? A spark fanned to life in the depths of her aching heart, a wisp of anger among all the ashes of mourning. "You're the one who has broken her heart, Uriel. *You*." She took plenty of responsibility upon her shoulders in life—for her sisters, her family, their futures. But she wouldn't take this.

Riding that flame, small as it was, she turned back to the camp and strode off, trusting that Kapriel would either keep up or catch up. She had to get home before she crumbled.

CHAPTER FOURTEEN

G od had known.

That was the thought that kept Mahlah company under the stars that night, when she'd crawled silently out of their tent and slipped a minute's walk into the wilderness. In some ways, it was a ridiculous thought. Of *course* God had known— God knew everything, saw everything. It was no revelation to Him that Uriel's service to Him ended at his lips.

Still, she sat with the epiphany for the space of many heartbeats, letting it sink in. God had known that Uriel wasn't faithful. He had known it when He said Mahlah and her sisters could inherit on behalf of their father...and He'd known it when He added that they must marry within their tribe.

It had been for the sake of all Israel, yes. To guarantee fairness. But it had been for *her* too. For her best.

Not some kind of test to help her decide if she valued love above responsibility and legacy. Nor one to force her to choose obedience even when she cried out that it was unfair.

He'd said it because He knew that Uriel had crossed a dangerous line, and He wanted to protect her from the consequences. He'd said it because it was for her best good. He'd said it because He loved her.

Love. How could it be both a beautiful thing and yet so foolish? How could it create such a strong bond between her parents, yet have made her so weak and stupid that she'd nearly tossed away the greatest promise, the greatest trust, to chase after something that would have destroyed her along with it?

How could she want to curse it yet still crave it, all at once?

At least the tears weren't pushing their way up and out anymore. She'd held them in check all day, not wanting to explain everything to her younger sisters. It had been enough, she hoped, to have told them her decision.

She wouldn't marry Uriel. She'd marry someone within the tribe. Eventually.

They'd exchanged a few looks, opened their mouths to press for answers, but something in her expression must have stopped them. Or No'ah's glare and shake of the head had done it. One or the other, or a combination of both. In either case, they'd merely nodded, had each taken a turn giving her a hug, and had gone about their duties as she did her own.

She'd asked No'ah to forbid all guests entrance today, but also to let all the busybodies of the tribe know about her decision. Telling a few select women and men would guarantee that everyone would know by morning.

Then she had simply kept moving. Cooking with one sister, sewing with another, tidying up with a third. She'd practiced the song Hoglah wanted at her wedding on her harp while Kap—who didn't count as a guest—played his pipe and Izik teased a rhythm from his drum. No'ah, Milcah, and Tirzah had worked on the new lyrics they were writing for the celebration, singing along with the music sometimes, pausing to consider new wording at others.

Then, finally, it had been time to retire. She'd crawled into her bedding, held herself in a tight ball until No'ah's breathing had gone slow and regular, then had let the tears come.

She'd expected a torrent, one she'd have to fight to keep silent. Instead, they'd been a steady stream, shaking her shoulders but never demanding breath she didn't have. Then they were spent, and she wasn't. She was wide awake, left to stare at the dark tent above her.

How long had she lain there? An hour...three? Eventually she'd given up and risen, had sneaked out here into the night.

No'ah would chide her if she knew. Kap and Izik would growl and...well, come out with her, most likely. Remind her of how foolish it was to be out at night, alone, when there were not only raiders about who had killed Abba but men in her own camp not above violence if it meant securing her double inheritance on top of their own.

Hence the knife balanced on her knee and the bow and arrows on her back.

And the senses on high alert, even through all her thoughts. She heard the night bird way off in the trees, the rustle of some small animal in the grass. She saw the dance of moonlight on wing and the rocking of the boughs in the breeze.

She knew where the members of the night watch were on this western side of camp, tracked their pacing to and from each checkpoint, and was aware of it the very moment one spotted her and started her way.

Her hand curled around the handle of her knife. She didn't throw it with quite the accuracy that she boasted with a bow, but she knew how to wield it in close quarters, if necessary.

When the full moon's light revealed that it was Cozbi, of all people, walking toward her, she wondered if *necessary* could well be the case.

He recognized her at nearly the same moment. She could see it in the way his posture changed. He went from mildly curious and purposeful—no doubt ready to tell whatever foolish person was out here alone to get back to the safety of camp—to...a different kind of purposeful. There was a hitch in his stride, and then it took on a new movement. Nearly a swagger but not exactly.

She kept her hand on her knife, the knife on her knee. He would either see it or he wouldn't.

When he was a few steps away, he spoke, moonlight gleaming on his teeth. "Well, well. If it isn't Mahlah, out here all alone. Where are your pet guardians, hmm? Kapriel? Izik?"

"Behind you." She said it mildly and had to bite back a smile when he spun, scanned the darkness. They *were* behind him...in their tent. Sleeping, she hoped.

He muttered something ugly sounding when he faced her again. Came a step closer. "What are you doing out here? Meeting your precious Benjaminite?"

She shifted the blade just a bit so that it caught the moon's light, winked it back. He stopped. She smiled, though it felt as sharp as the knife. "No. I won't see him again, except in passing. I'll marry within the tribe—the Lord knows what is best for me."

His posture shifted again. The threatening hunch of his shoulders relaxed, and his smile went from mocking to inviting. "Ah. Good. And good that you didn't come out here unprotected. Clearly you're a woman of sense and wisdom."

Funny how a compliment from him made her grip the knife all the tighter. She stood. Partly because she might as well go home, if her solitude was over. And partly because she didn't like feeling at a disadvantage around him. Better to be on his level. Face to face, eye to eye. Better to remind him that she was a daughter of Zelophehad, schooled by a father instead of a mother. She made a show of repositioning her bow on her shoulder.

On anyone else, his amused smile would have invited a return one from her. "You really *did* come out here prepared."

"As you say—I'm a woman of sense and wisdom. And one never knows where threats may come from." Perhaps she shouldn't have leveled her pointed look on him—but she did.

He stiffened again. "I get the feeling, Mahlah, that you don't much like me."

She opened her mouth, ready to agree, but he kept on talking, obviously not caring what she said.

"Which is a shame. Because I'm the best choice you have for a husband. My father's herds are so vast that he'll require an equally vast portion of land to care for them. And my older brother—he's sick. He doesn't want anyone to know, but there's a growth in his abdomen. It's unlikely he'll live out the year."

He said it as if losing his brother would be a good thing, a benefit. As if all it meant was getting that firstborn's portion and not losing a *brother*. She sidestepped away from him and aimed her feet toward camp.

He kept pace beside her. "Our lands are bound to be close, given that our fathers were cousins. If we were to combine all that my father will get with your firstborn portion, we'll be the richest family in Manasseh—in all Israel."

She shook her head and opened her stride. "I really don't care about that, Cozbi."

"Of course you do—because you're a woman of sense and wisdom." He reached for her arm.

She pulled it away, leaped a step to the side, and raised her knife-hand to chest height, parallel with the ground. "The last time you touched me, you left bruises. I'll thank you not to try it again."

He looked more irritated than cowed. "I saved you from a terrible match that day—you ought to be thanking me, not harping over the fact that my grip was too strong in my excitement."

Maybe she should, at that. But she wasn't ready to admit it. "And what would you have done—or tried to do, anyway—if I hadn't said I'd broken things off with Uriel? Hmm? Out there a few minutes ago? What would you have tried, what bruises would you have left in your *excitement* tonight?"

He lifted his chin, opened his mouth. She was curious, she could admit, as to what he might say, and she could see by the light of the moon that something darker than night still lurked in his eyes.

But before he could utter a word, a shout came up from the edge of camp. And then everything turned to chaos.

No'ah awoke with the instant feeling of aloneness, her senses long trained to alert her to anytime Mahlah left their partition. Usually, it meant morning crept up on them and No'ah had better rise too. When it came while darkness still ruled at the tent's edges, it meant either someone was sick or Mahlah had enjoyed a cup of tea too close to bedtime.

She sat up, listening, but she didn't hear her sister move toward where they stored the chamber pot, and there were no sounds of the younger girls moaning or retching.

Just the whisper of the tent flap moving under gentle, secretive hands.

She slid out of bed and hurried toward the main entrance, breathing a bit easier when she saw that Mahlah's weapons were gone with her, wherever she went. No'ah grabbed hers too and ducked outside.

Given all the practice she'd had lately following potential suitors, tracking her sister without being seen didn't require much work. She didn't leave the shadows of the tents, even, just watched as Mahlah moved toward the place where they'd had the tribal campfire forty-two days ago, watched her sit.

She could understand her sister needing time, solitude, the peace that only a star-studded night sky could give.

She also knew that leaving her out there unguarded and alone wasn't an option. Keeping her gaze locked on the small bump in the landscape that was Mahlah's head, No'ah tiptoed past the tent between hers and Seth's, moved to the side where she knew Izik slept, and scratched at the fabric.

It wouldn't be the first time one of them had awakened the other in the middle of the night, but usually it was so they could get into mischief. Play a prank on someone that required darkness, pick all the berries before other children could get to them in the daylight, or whatever else had seemed so important to their minds as little ones.

If he didn't hear her, she'd go from scratching to humming.

But he did, as usual. He cleared his throat in a way that would sound natural to his family but which, to her, meant "Give me a minute."

A minute later, he was ghosting up beside her, still rubbing his eyes. "What is it?"

She pointed out to the fields, drifting a few steps away from the tents. "Mahlah went out there. Just to sit and think, I imagine. I didn't want to leave her alone, but I had a feeling you wouldn't approve of me being out here alone either."

"I much prefer keeping you company, without question." He led her a few more steps away, enough that they could at least speak in a normal whisper, rather than the barest breath they'd been using. Then he stopped them and sat down. "And good instincts."

Her eyes scanned the long line of tents, stretching endlessly, it seemed, both north and south. "Who has our watch tonight?"

"Gavriel and Cozbi—hence the good instincts." He yawned, but she could practically see his senses sharpening, alertness taking the place of slumber as each second eased by.

For perhaps a quarter of an hour, nothing stirred, and they sat in comfortable silence. Then one of the watchmen came into view from the north, ambling along the length of tents of Manasseh, eyes scanning the horizon. She'd identified him as Cozbi just a second before he seemed to spot Mahlah. She watched him stiffen, then move into the field.

"Cozbi," she murmured, since Izik's attention was southward.

He nodded, glanced that way, but then looked south again. "There's movement out there, off in the distance. Near the folds."

"Probably just our shepherds." There were always men from each tribe watching over the flocks by night, just as there were others patrolling the perimeter of camp.

Izik's hum didn't sound like agreement.

Following his gaze for a few seconds told her why. The shepherds, if they had cause to return to camp or chase an animal into the night, would be moving with confidence, boldness even. If they were chasing off a predator, they'd be making themselves big and moving quickly.

The forms he'd spotted were clearly human, but they were slinking along the ground in a crouch. Coming from the glen nearer the camp of Benjamin than their own.

Her stomach tightened at the thought of what she'd seen in that glen yesterday. Surely that, more than any present danger, was what made her nerves tingle and her stomach go tight. She gripped her twin daggers, one in each hand, and kept moving her gaze between the more distant figures and Cozbi and Mahlah.

She couldn't hear what her sister said to their cousin, though she clearly had a handle on the situation. No'ah breathed a little easier when Mahlah stood, the outline of her weapons clearly visible in the night. Good.

The crouched figures were closer but largely blending in now with the terrain behind them. Had she not known where to track their movement, she could have missed them easily.

Children, she hoped. Picking the berries before their friends could in the morning. Adolescents, playing pranks on their cousins or rivals. Perhaps even a man and woman stealing a moonlit kiss—risky, but she'd take that over the other option that kept pummeling her mind.

Bandits. Thieves. Murderers. Raiders.

Mahlah and Cozbi were striding back toward camp, their voices coming in indistinct waves of sound to her ears. She was aware of them stopping, of Cozbi reaching out and Mahlah sidestepping him, of her sister raising her arm in a defensive posture.

But her gaze was locked now on the shadows. They were moving closer. And they stood tall now—taller than children, more fearsome than adolescents with the weapons they raised.

Izik flew into action half a second before No'ah did the same, both of them bursting into the open, screams on their lips. "Attack! Raiders!"

His shout, hers, tangled together.

"The horn!" Izik shouted, aiming it at Cozbi and Mahlah. Or, no, Cozbi. Cozbi was on the watch. He'd have a horn at his side to blow in case an alarm needed to be sounded. "Blow the alarm!" Even as he shouted, he was whipping an arrow out of the quiver he'd had on his back and nocking it into his bow.

Had she been any good with a bow, No'ah would have chided herself for not bringing her own. She had only her twin daggers, and she adjusted her grip on them and ran as fast as her legs would pump, the blood buzzing in her ears.

After a moment of shock, another moment lost as both Mahlah and Cozbi spun to face the wilderness, Cozbi finally raised the horn to his lips and blew. Mahlah quickly sheathed her knife and reached for bow and arrow, sending one flying toward the quickly approaching intruders.

The strangers had loosed arrows of their own, one of which caught in the fabric of No'ah tunic as she ran. She breathed her gratitude to God for the miss and kept running.

One of them screamed when someone's arrow hit him— Mahlah's? Izik's?—but he didn't fall. The other threw something at Izik that winked wickedly in the moonlight. Iz lunged to the side to evade it, rolled, popped back up to his feet. The third and final man sent another arrow flying that clattered against a rock behind her.

Other horns were sending the alarm onward now, other shouts coming from behind them. The strangers were reaching for each other, tugging, redirecting. As one, they turned and fled.

No'ah would have kept running after them, but Izik stopped and held out an arm to stop her too. She did, breath heaving in and out with a pleasant burn. "I didn't even get to use my knives."

"And praise the Lord for that." He still had an arrow in his bow, still had it up and was following the running men with his aim, but he didn't let it fly.

Mahlah and Cozbi both came to a halt beside them, Mahlah's bow also raised, Cozbi gripping a long, nasty-looking blade. All attention stayed focused on the raiders until they vanished from sight.

When No'ah turned, she saw that men had emerged from the line of tents all up and down the camp, weapons and torches in hand. It would be enough to keep the raiders from coming back, without question. Three men might sneak up looking for the opportunity to steal or kill, but they weren't going to take on an entire nation.

It seemed the others running out spotted the distant, armed figures and shouted the information back, because when Seth slowed from his run and joined them a minute later, he didn't ask his son what was going on. He had an arrow in his hands, having apparently picked it up from behind them. An arrow with three double rows of fletching and a feather trailing behind it. He said, "How did you know to come out here so early?"

Izik gave that little-boy grin that somehow didn't look at odds against the weapon in his hands and glanced at No'ah. "Good instincts."

CHAPTER FIFTEEN

No'ah pulled another berry free of its vine and dropped it into her basket. The sun warmed her head and back, tempting her to set aside the chore, the basket, and the berries and curl up on that rock there instead. To let the gurgle of the river and the song of the birds lull her into a much-needed nap.

By the time she and Mahlah had returned home, explained to their sisters what had happened, and gotten themselves all settled again, the night had been half spent. Even then, her whole body had felt abuzz, light, bright, awake. She kept replaying the preceding events in her mind over and over, again and again, as if some new detail could emerge.

Eventually, she'd fallen asleep. For an hour. Perhaps two. Then daylight spilled onto the world again, the camp woke up, and *everyone* was buzzing so loudly, she couldn't ignore them even with a pillow over her head.

Mahlah had been merciful though and sent her out for berry picking. Izik had assigned himself as her guard, even though he probably had better things to do. But then, no one was going out alone just now. And children were being kept close to their immas' tents, those mothers too frightened by the close encounter last night to let them run free as usual. Which meant no competition for the berries.

She grinned, largely because of how she'd thought about those children and berries the night before. But also because nothing terrible had happened last night. They'd scared off the raiders. Kept her sister, all her sisters, safe. Kept *everyone* safe.

With a yawn, she set the basket down and stretched. The sunshine felt delicious on her face.

Izik poured the berries he'd picked from his small bowl into her larger basket but then paused on his way back up, frowning. "Did you catch your tunic on a thorn?"

"Hmm?" She looked down, saw the tear he'd noticed near her knee, and leaned down to touch it. She'd forgotten about the rip in all the other excitement last night, otherwise she would have mended it or changed into her spare garment before coming out here. "Oh, that. No. It's where the enemy's arrow missed me last night."

"What?" Izik snapped back upright, his eyes a raging inferno. "You were hit?"

"No." She said it slowly, deliberately. "I did *not* get hit. Hence when it *missed* me."

He leveled an accusing finger at the rip. "But it hit your clothes."

"And my clothes are not *me*. Hence—"

"And you didn't bother mentioning this? That an enemy arrow came within a fraction of a measure of hitting you?"

She spread her hands, eyes wide. "I'd forgotten! It hardly mattered in all the excitement. Because it *missed*."

He looked as if he was about to erupt. In more words, likely. Shouting them, quite possibly. She wouldn't even have been surprised if he'd stormed off, hefted a few large rocks into the river just for the exertion, and then stomped back.

Instead he spun, shoving agitated, berry-stained fingers into his hair, pivoted three steps away, and stalked right back. He pointed his pink-tipped finger at her nose. "You're not a soldier. Not a night watchman."

"And I don't want to be." She wrapped her own fingers around the one trying to make her eyes cross and lowered it. "It isn't as though I went looking for trouble, Iz. But what do you expect me to do when it finds me? Run screaming the other direction?"

"That's what many girls would do."

"Not Zelophehad's daughters."

He snorted and pulled his finger free. "How well I know that. You're all going to be the death of me."

The irritation had started the way irritations usually did— just a minor annoyance, to be smoothed away with a brush of fingers. But the more he said, the worse it grew.

Oh, she knew that he was just as exhausted as she was and that tomorrow, neither the tear from the arrow nor the fact that she'd been out facing down the enemy would have bothered him so much.

That did nothing to mollify her now. She planted her hands on her hips and lifted her chin. "Well, lucky for you, we won't be your problem much longer. You'll have us all married off soon enough, and then we'll be someone *else's* headache to manage."

"The younger ones, yes. But it's you and Mahlah who think you can just go out by yourselves in the middle of the night—"

"I did not! I fetched *you!*"

"—and the two of you who refuse to just fall in love with the right people like you're supposed to."

Of all the ridiculous accusations to lob at her. "If you recall, Mahlah *did* fall in love—"

"With the absolute wrong man."

She couldn't exactly argue with that at this point. Even if he did look absolutely infuriating as he stood there glowering down at her, his arms folded across his chest. "And why worry about me? You already said you had my perfect husband picked out, so just point him out to me and let's get on with it. I'm ready to meet him!"

He'd call her bluff, of course. She hadn't given any thought at all to preparing her own heart for a husband—how could she, with everything happening with her sisters? Her every thought had been consumed with Mahlah's tragedy and Hoglah's joy, with Milcah's new way of smiling and Tirzah's delight in new love springing up.

He stepped toward her, took her hand—something he'd done a thousand times before. She expected him to tug her into motion, pull her down the path and back toward camp. Calling the bluff. Forcing her to admit that the thought of learning how to like, even love, someone else made all those bees inside her veins buzz and hum until she couldn't hear anything over them.

Only, he didn't move, didn't pull her along. He just stood there, inches away, holding her hand gently in his. Looking down into her eyes, his own still ablaze but with a very different-looking fire. "All right," he said, voice a tight whisper. "Here he is."

Her heart was a hive, its noise too loud to make any sense of anything. All she could push past her lips was a half-hearted "What?"

He took her other hand too. "I love you, No'ah. I've always loved you."

"I know. I've been like a sister—"

"No. Not like a sister. Not for a long time." He moved even closer, somehow, a shift that made her have to tilt her head back to keep looking him in the eye, that let her feel the sun's heat radiating off him, that brought the scent of berries and spring and Izik to her nose.

"But…" She didn't know what her objection was, just that it made no sense. "You've known me all our lives."

"And mean to love you till the end of them."

The buzzing was in her throat. Or maybe her eyes. Or in the fingers he held. "How could you love me?"

"Because I know you." His thumbs stroked over her knuckles. "Inside and out. And there's no other woman in the world for me. Only you. I've known it forever."

Had his fingers not held hers captive with their gentle grasp, she might have slapped at him. "Then why haven't you said anything before now?"

"You weren't ready." His larynx bobbed when he swallowed. "I made Abba promise never to arrange a marriage with anyone else. Your Abba knew too, and approved, but…but you had to want me too."

She wanted to cry. And laugh. And scream. And curl up against him and let him hold her for the rest of eternity. Was that love? She swallowed down a few of the bees. "And do I? Am I ready?"

For the first time in the conversation—no, for the first time ever—uncertainty wobbled its way over Izik's face. "I hope so. If I've ruined it all now, after waiting all these years, I..."

Was he handsome? She knew his face too well to say. She knew other girls darted looks at him and Kapriel both, and giggled behind their hands. She knew she liked watching his mischievous smile sneak onto his lips. She knew she never tired of looking his way and guessing at his thoughts and knowing he read hers just as easily.

She felt safest, calmest, most excited by his side. Her fingers felt most at home, able to still, when his held them. When she had a thought buzzing about that she couldn't quite lay hold of, he could always put it into words for her.

Maybe, all along, that was why she'd never wanted to think about marrying anyone. Because she couldn't bear to imagine a life in which Izik wasn't the one at her side—but she hadn't imagined he'd ever look at her like that.

Like he was doing now. Like if she gave the word, he'd float off into the clouds from happiness. Or if she gave another, he'd shatter to pieces.

A breath shuddered from her lungs, chased by the shadow of a laugh. "Do you *always* have to be right?"

His lips twitched, though the smile ran away again before it bloomed full, too wary. "I'll trade every other occasion, if I can just be right about this."

"I think...I think you are." The words were easier to say than she thought they'd be, even if a little frisson of fear still waggled up her spine. Because what if they were wrong? This wasn't a conversation they could just decide to ignore and let life go back to normal. There would be no normal after this, not like before.

For that matter, what if they were right?

Either way, everything changed when they left these wild berry brambles. Either their friendship would be over or...or it would transform into something new. Bigger.

He let go of her fingers with one hand, and she felt the loss of his touch keenly enough to make her breath catch. Then it held when his hand rested instead against her cheek. Eyes still locked on hers, he drew her closer. Or bent down. Or both. Closing the distance, making her heart pound harder and faster with each inch closer he drew.

The first touch of his lips on hers was honey and sunlight and flowers and...and home. Her now-free hand lifted to rest against his heart, and she could feel it pounding every bit as hard as hers. For *her*. Because he loved her. Because he knew the risk of saying it too and had waited years—years!—to do so, so that she would be ready.

Yesterday, she would have said she wasn't. Today, now, here, in his arms—his arms had somehow moved around her and pulled her tight—she could have leaped straight into which-ever tomorrow would make her his wife.

Eventually he pulled away, though she couldn't have said whether it was seconds or days later. He drew in a shaking breath. He rested his forehead against hers, his eyes closed. "If this is all a dream, don't let anyone wake me up. Ever."

She chuckled and pinched his arm, laughing more at his flinch. "Not a dream. Not yours, anyway. It could still be mine, I suppose."

The eyes that had flown open at her pinch narrowed at her. But his perfectly troublemaking smile was back on his lips. "You didn't know to dream about this."

"Doesn't mean it didn't just come to me. Out of the blue. Flash of epiphany."

"Hmm." He kissed her again, quick and hard, and then drew in a deep breath. "Will you be my wife, Little Bee?"

She pursed her lips. And curled her fingers tight in the shoulder of his tunic. "Well. Perhaps, if you can convince my uncles to grant their approval. Though they *are* very insistent that we all take our time and make certain we really *know* our suitors, so don't be surprised if—"

He tickled her side, and she squealed and laughed and pressed closer instead of pulling away. "All right, I surrender! I'll marry you!"

His hands slid up her back, anchoring her against him. "Quickly."

Quickly sounded good. Already her lips were yearning for another taste of his, and being this close to him made her breath flutter away. She nodded and rested her head against his chest, where the rapid thudding of his heart lit a smile in her own. "You know, if you'd just told me sooner that I loved you, we could be married already."

A chuckle rumbled in his chest. "Don't think I didn't consider saying it a thousand times. But if you'd run away from me instead of into my arms...I couldn't live with that." He rested his chin on her head. "You're worth the wait."

She closed her eyes, tried to commit each and every one of his honey-sweet words to memory so that she could whisper them later to her sisters. Tell them how he'd turned her hornet into a honeybee with just the right thoughts. How he'd made her realize that he'd held her heart forever. She held him tighter. Squeezed her eyes shut. "I'm sorry it took me so long."

"I'm not. Had we married before your abba's death, you wouldn't have been there for your sisters the way they needed you to be. And since then...you had to focus on them. That was right. Good."

Gracious, was it any wonder she'd never considered any other man? How could anyone ever hope to compare to Izik? She pulled away, catching his hands as she escaped them. "Come on. Let's go talk to Abiram."

He kissed her once more first, then scooped up their berries. They ran down the hill with their fingers entwined, and the very fact that such a thing was nothing new, nothing to make people look twice at them when they reached groups of friends and neighbors and family, made her wonder if everyone else had known this was the inevitable outcome of their closeness. If she was the only one in Israel who hadn't seen the truth of it long ago.

If so, she could swallow down the affront to her pride and laugh. Because here they were, not just together but truly together. Soon to be one.

They went straight to her family's tent, and the smile she hadn't been able to wipe off her lips grew when she saw that Abiram was inside too, standing beside Mahlah while she scoured a pot more forcefully than it really required.

It looked as though tempers were short here too. Well, perhaps she could brighten the day a bit. "Abiram, I'm glad you're here."

"No'ah—finally." Abiram spun to face her, face set in determined lines and hands planted on his hips. "I'll tell you what I just told Mahlah. You know I want what's best for you, that we all do, and that we want to honor your abba's wishes—but the situation is becoming too volatile. Too dangerous. We need all of you married quickly, for your own safety."

She could alleviate the concern about *her* easily enough, but...

"What's happened?" Izik spoke before she did, of course, taking the very question from her mouth. He slid the basket of berries onto the work bench beside Mahlah, who didn't even look up in thanks or acknowledgment.

Odd, for Mahlah. Her sister's jaw looked clenched so tight it must ache, even as she bit out, "Cozbi."

That didn't exactly clear it up. No'ah looked to Abiram again.

He heaved a sigh. "He's saying...implying...that Mahlah was out there last night to keep a tryst."

"With *him*," Mahlah said, looking as though she'd like to spit.

"That's ridiculous!" No'ah surged closer to her sister.

Abiram lifted his hands. "Of course it is. But without witnesses saying otherwise—"

"I'm a witness! I followed her out the minute she left the tent. I saw her walk to the spot where we gathered for Abba's funeral remembrance. I saw her sit. I saw him spot her and walk over and saw her immediately get up and start walking back."

"As did I," Izik added with a somber nod. "We can bear witness that nothing was exchanged between them but a few words."

Abiram nodded. Then frowned. "And what were the two of *you* doing out there in the middle of the night?"

No'ah blinked at him. "Like I just said. I followed Mahlah— I wanted to make sure she was safe. But I got Izik first, because I wanted us to be *safe*."

That didn't seem to mollify him. He raised a hand, pointed a finger at her. "And how exactly did you get *Izik* without waking the rest of his family? Because they didn't know anything until the alarms sounded." Not waiting for an answer, he shook his head and mumbled something she didn't catch. Then, "Sometimes, No'ah, it seems you haven't a scrap of logic. Don't you realize you can't just go about at night with an unmarried man? Unless *you* want rumors abounding too, then—"

"I don't mind. Let the rumors abound. Draw up the betrothal agreement now, and we'll just stave them all off."

He rolled his eyes. Actually rolled his eyes, like one of his six-year-old sons. "I was only warning you of what *could* happen. And really, Izik, I would expect better of you. I know you only have the girls' best interest at heart, but why didn't you wake your father to go with you? To protect No'ah's reputation?"

His lips twitched. "Guilty. Draw up the betrothal agreement."

Abiram opened his mouth as if to argue again, then paused and turned his frown from one of them to the other. "Wait. Are you...serious?"

From somewhere behind them, Tirzah snorted. "Well *that* took long enough. I was beginning to think you'd never speak up, Iz."

The glare he shot her youngest sister was about as menacing as a newborn lamb. "I was giving her time to realize she can't live without me."

"And had you waited any longer, Abiram would have forced your hand by threatening to choose for her." Tirzah breezed into view, a grin on her lips and manna cakes in her hands, ready for the fire. "I'm only saying, you waited until the last possible moment."

No'ah chuckled at their antics. And smiled at Abiram. And took some consolation in the fact that both he and Mahlah looked as dumbfounded by the revelation as she had been, even if Tirzah had known. "Quite serious. Unless you disapprove?"

He laughed at the joke. "I'll speak with Seth straightaway." His gaze flicked to Izik. "Will he be surprised?"

That crooked, heart-melting smile. "No. Nor was he when I first mentioned it five years ago."

Five years ago! They'd been sixteen, and he'd known very well she meant to wait, along with all her sisters, until Tirzah was of age before she married. But still he'd known. And spoken to his father—and hers. To Mahlah and Tirzah, she said, "Abba knew too," in a tone of voice that said, *Isn't he as sweet as honey?*

Tirzah chuckled. Mahlah, though. Mahlah's expression was still working on shaking loose the frown inspired by Cozbi. It had moved to neutral through the exchange, and shocked. And now a slow smile bloomed. Abandoning her pot, she moved over to No'ah and wrapped her in a tight embrace. "You love him. I can see it in your eyes. How could we have missed that all this time?"

No'ah laughed. "I have no idea. I'm just glad I know it now." But when she pulled away, the situation they'd walked in on flew back into focus. Her smile faded, and the shadows under her sister's eyes struck her like a blow. "Mahlah? What are you going to do?"

CHAPTER SIXTEEN

What are you going to do?

W*hat are you going to do?* The words echoed in Mahlah's heart long after No'ah spoke them. They'd been echoing there an hour before she came in, flushed and sunny and glowing with love, not just berry-picking, apparently. They'd been echoing since the moment she heard the whisper when she went to fetch water from the river, from one aunt or cousin's wife to another. About *her*. And…him.

What are you going to do?

Something. She grabbed up their empty waterskin and looped it over her shoulder. "I'll get the evening's water," she said to the tent at large, not knowing or caring which of her family heard and acknowledged it. She couldn't let this go unanswered. She couldn't let Cozbi's greed be what dictated her life. She wouldn't.

But that determination didn't actually give her an answer to how to fix it. How to unravel the rumors he was carefully spreading throughout the tribe. She stomped out of the tent, toward the river, one of many women making the trek. Far from alone, with the whole tribe around to see that she wasn't out in secret meeting a man.

Gossiping about whether she'd really been kissing Cozbi when she'd been considering a betrothal to a Benjaminite.

It was in her favor that No'ah and Izik had witnessed their entire interaction, yes. But some people would dismiss their testimony, saying they were just trying to cover up her sin.

That was the true stealth of his lie, though—he wasn't accusing her and hence himself of *sin*. Just of the opportunity for it. Of taking a step that could have led to it. And he had *confessed* it to his own father because of his desire for a clean conscience, he'd said—in the hearing of his mother and aunt, two of the biggest gossips in Israel.

What are you going to do?

She chose a spot on the banks of the river well away from anyone else and plunged her waterskin beneath the water. It gurgled, bubbled, and didn't fill nearly as quickly as it should have because she didn't bother to angle it to let the air out. Let it take three times as long as it should. That would merely give the icy waters time to numb her hand and, if she was fortunate, cool her raging temper too.

"Mahlah."

She flicked her gaze up, saw Kapriel crouching a few feet away, his face earnest and concerned, and looked down again. Fury made her tremble. Not with Kap, just with *this*. All of it. She ought to have been greeting him with a laugh and a shouted, playful demand to know if he'd realized Izik had been determined to marry No'ah all this time. Or she should have been able to mourn with him over the loss of Uriel. They should have been able to talk about anything or nothing and think nothing of it.

Instead, she knew this too would be about Cozbi. Abiram's insistence that she needed to be betrothed and then married, *fast*. That if she wasn't, that wretched man *would* find a way to force her into it. With expectation and tribal pressure if not from an actual physical attack that she might be able to fend off.

"You don't need to check on me, Kap." Of course, her tone belied her words. He'd hear how angry she was, and it was something she dwelled in so infrequently that of *course* he would be concerned.

"I'm not. I know you're not all right. How could you be?"

Her shoulders sagged just enough that the nozzle tilted and the skin filled in earnest. Why was it always worse when someone saw her clearly? With Abiram making demands for her own safety and her sisters wild with anger on her behalf, she could stay unmoved from this strangely comfortable place of righteous indignation.

But the moment he saw through it to the pain beneath, she deflated. "In a few months or years, this won't matter. I'll have sorted it out. All my sisters will be happy. We'll forget it ever happened."

"That doesn't solve the problem."

She breathed a mirthless laugh and sat down on the bank of the river. "I don't know what will solve it."

"I do."

His tone was that resigned, heavy one that warned her he was about to say something utterly reasonable that she wouldn't like. He sat too, a foot away, and focused his gaze on the clear, gurgling water. "We can marry."

She was tempted to laugh the same dry laugh again but didn't. It would be redundant. And perhaps offensive. "Are you going to try to tell me you've loved me all along, like Iz and No'ah?"

"No." He let out a long breath, the gold of the sun, an hour from setting, strong on his face. "I wish that were true. But the truth is simply that you're not just a cousin, you're one of my dearest friends. I've always thought of you as a sister—but you're not. And you're in a dangerous situation, one where someone who would make you miserable is trying to force you into something that would last a lifetime. I can't let that happen, and I have it in my power to stop it. So I will. If you'll allow me."

She looked at the water too, letting the words wash over her heart the way the water did the toes she dangled in it. It was too cold to sit here like this for long, but the shards of pain were comforting somehow. Like his offer. It proved she was something more than a pawn to be used by the likes of Cozbi, even if neither was comfortable. "You don't want to get married yet."

"It wasn't my intention, no. But when do we ever get to dictate the course of our own lives? When does anything? Even this river will deviate from its straight path when it hits ground too hard to cut through." He motioned to the wide bend of it, in which Israel had made its camp. "We are created things, just like this. Not the masters of our own lives. We don't control where we end up or how we get there. We can only keep flowing, keep moving, keeping doing the thing we were made for."

It was a truth too beautiful to argue with. Words her soul needed to hear.

Even though Abba had tried so hard to let her chart the course of her own life, it wasn't his to grant. God Himself had set her feet on a different path. One that led here. Right here. Where the rocks of life seemed unbreakable. Where the waters of her world crashed and beat upon them, made her scream at the injustice.

But Kapriel was right, whether his particular solution was or not. When rivers couldn't flow straight, they turned instead. Or they formed lakes. Or they crashed over cliffs. They changed and they adapted and then kept moving, always moving.

She would have to do the same. In the face of the heart that Uriel broke and the injustice of Cozbi's lies, she wouldn't cower or rant. She would shift. Somehow. She nodded.

Kapriel drew in a breath. "Does that nod mean you'll marry me, or that you're simply granting the point about the river?"

He knew her well, she'd give him that. Her lips turned up just a bit. "River."

"Somehow I suspected that. Think about it, at least, will you? I'm not the worst option in Manasseh."

That brought her gaze over to him and made her smile grow another fraction. If she were trying to convince a friend to accept a betrothal with him, she could have listed his every virtue, his strengths, all the things that made him Kapriel. That made him, as he'd said of her, one of her dearest friends. "That's the point, Kap. I don't want to trap you for life in a marriage you offered simply to save me from Cozbi's schemes. You deserve better. Someday, when you're ready."

He abandoned the view of the river and, shaking his head, repositioned himself to face her. "Let's think it through. I've never had the goal your abba swore by, of waiting until my heart is stolen by some pretty maiden. My assumption has always been that when the time came, I'd marry someone I liked, who liked me, whose family and mine got along, who would complement me, and I her." He raised his brows.

She rolled her eyes. "Yes, fine, I meet those criteria."

"Next. I assumed that she wouldn't love me so fully either at the start, but that there would be affection. I assumed that, because we chose to build a life together, love would bloom. Like it did for *my* parents, for our aunts and uncles. Isn't that, in fact, what happened to Izik and No'ah, but when they were still young and unwed?"

She tilted her head, watched the way he spoke as much as she listened to the words. He meant every one of them. There was no reserve in his manner, no hesitation in his movements. He had decided that this was the best course, and he was flowing toward it like a river. "I suppose it is."

"And you don't have to doubt whether their marriage will be a good one, because they *know* each other. Better than anyone else in the world does." He scooted an inch closer. "We know each other that well too. And you know very well that our parents always hoped we would seek a match. That Abiram would have acted on it in the Shadow's stead if No'ah hadn't made him promise to respect the Shadow's wishes."

She lifted her brows. "And if Abiram had decided *not* to let us choose our husbands for ourselves, if he had approached your father about the two of us—what would you have said? Assuming," she added when she saw the spark of objection in his eyes, "that Uriel was not an option."

He turned his hands palms up and shrugged. "How can I know? I likely would have tried to explain my desire to wait until our battles were won. But if Abba had insisted that this was the better option—if he'd perhaps pointed out that we would have time to start a family whose well-being I could then guarantee for generations with my portion of our inheritance, even if I *were* to die in battle...I could have been swayed. I could well have decided that starting a life beside my best friend now sounded better than maybe finding someone later I liked *almost* as much."

Her toes were numb. But he'd warmed her insides a bit. Not with the kind of excitement she'd felt when she thought of Uriel, of becoming his wife, of having his children. It wasn't that flame of anticipation at all, just...a comfort. Knowing that he might always have chosen to be by her side.

Because it wasn't a bad fate. Far from it. Of the choices she had in Manasseh, she couldn't think of anyone she would prefer to him. She just...couldn't be sure. Her gaze dropped to his upturned palms. Rough with work. Capable of defending her. Quick to comfort. She'd put hers in them often enough over the years. She knew she could trust him and that he'd never let her down.

She just didn't know if the love for a friend who'd felt like a brother all her life would ever become the kind of love her father had wanted for her so fiercely. If Abba were here, if Cozbi's lies had never been uttered, if Uriel had still been discovered and dismissed...would he ever let her marry Kapriel?

Without that bolt of realization that No'ah had experienced today about Izik? Or would he look her in the eye and say, "Wait, my precious song. Wait for the love that will carry you away. You won't be sorry."

Kapriel let out a long breath. "You're still not convinced."

A line of pain wove through his words, which lanced her in turn. "Kap—it isn't that I can think of any better option. It isn't that I don't love you all the more for being willing to do this for me. It isn't that we couldn't build a good life together. It's just..." She spread her own palms. "Abba."

He would know, did know what she meant. He pursed his lips, and a bit of humor sparked in his eyes again. "I like to think that even the Shadow would advise respect and affection here above manipulation and resentment."

"You mean that you're a better choice than Cozbi?" She snorted a laugh. "By leagues. That isn't the question." She squeezed her eyes shut. "What if you fall in love with someone else, later? Or I do? What if we meet our perfect match, the way my abba and imma did, only we're already bound to each other?"

"No. I won't grant your premise."

She opened her eyes again and found him with the same expression he'd worn yesterday, confronting Uriel about the Lord. "My premise?"

He tapped a finger to the opposite palm. "You're assuming that every person has only one other person they're capable of loving, and that the love renders them helpless to do anything but give in to it. I can't believe that's true. It happens sometimes, yes—but just as often as it happens, it fails. The people who lived by that passion decide they *don't* love the person anymore and find a new object of their desire."

Her cheeks flushed. "My abba—"

"Was not fickle. I'd never say he was. But that wasn't because he felt the bolt of lightning—it was because he chose to hold tight to it every day of his life. It wasn't the feeling, Mahlah. It was the choice. The *choice* that made your parents' marriage so successful, that made their love deepen day by day."

She dragged a long, deep breath into her lungs.

He leaned closer. "We may not have the lightning. But we can build a fire. And we can tend it. We can stoke it. We can choose, every day, to love each other. To love no one else. If attraction hits for another, we can choose to turn away. To come home and wrap our arms around each other. And God will honor that. Because He is not just the God of the lightning. He's the God of the river too. Of the earth and the sky and all the steady, slow-moving things. He's the God of Israel. And He loves us enough to want our best good. I can't believe He would lead us straight into temptation if we do our best to follow Him."

She nodded a slow, thoughtful nod. *Her best good.* She'd had to trust in that when the Lord had issued His commands for her and her sisters—and His wisdom and love had been proven at every turn. She had to trust Him now too. Trust that He was bigger than Cozbi's schemes. Certainly bigger than her own doubts and insecurities. "Thank you, Kapriel. Let me think and pray about this tonight and talk it over with my sisters."

Some of the tension seeped out of his shoulders, and he nodded. "Of course. I would say to take whatever time you need, and I mean that...but I don't know how much time we have."

"I know." She moved to stand, and he jumped to his feet too and reached to help her, taking the heavy waterskin. She gave the only answer she could give. "Tomorrow. I'll have a decision by tomorrow."

CHAPTER SEVENTEEN

No'ah scooped more manna into her bowl and hummed along with the song her younger sisters were singing in their tent. Her whole being felt light. Bright. Full of a joy that threatened to carry her away like a petal on the wind.

She kept her feet firmly planted, though, not even giving in to the urge to spin and dance her way through the morning's miracle. A stolen glance at her older sister served as her anchor. If No'ah felt made of sunshine and spring breezes today, Mahlah looked as though she was made of rock. Her every movement was slow, deliberate…heavy.

Kapriel would be coming after his morning chores. His parents would come with him. Abiram would arrive too, and quite possibly a few other uncles and aunts for good measure. And Mahlah would have to give them her choice. No'ah understood how heavy the burden felt to Mahlah, and it kept her own feet firmly planted.

Even though they wanted to dance—because Izik would come with his family. And he'd steal over to her side. His fingers would find hers, or he'd put an arm around her and draw her close. Perhaps, if they could find a moment of privacy, he would kiss her again.

Her stomach jittered deliciously at the thought.

Which, in turn, made something like guilt sink its teeth in her. She was happy—overjoyed—overflowing...but her sister wasn't. And so how could she be?

No'ah had tried to get her to talk through it all again last night, when they were in bed. Oh, they'd already analyzed every option and detail all together, as a family. All five sisters. They'd discussed it in calm voices, with logic and reason. And viewed solely from that place of logic and reason, the answer was obvious.

Mahlah should marry Kapriel.

But there had been no peace in her sister's expression, only heavy resignation. Or—was that the right word? It seemed it, at first glance, but the more she tried to pry into Mahlah's heart after everyone else had gone to bed, the more she wondered if it was something far darker.

Fear.

Fear of making the wrong choice. Fear of hurting one of her best friends. Fear of choosing a life that wasn't what Abba had wanted for her. Fear that nothing better waited. That the heaviness would simply become routine without ever lessening.

Fear that her marriage would be loss instead of gain. Burden rather than blessing.

No'ah adjusted her grip on her bowl, bit her lip to hold back the song still wanting to sing out, and scooped another handful of manna with as much calm as she could force into her fingers.

Shouldn't they be done by now? Gracious, five omers had never taken this long to gather, it seemed.

Beside her, Mahlah sighed and straightened, then turned her torso to face No'ah. "Stop."

Brows pulling toward her nose, No'ah straightened too. "Stop...what?"

Mahlah waved a hand to encompass No'ah's entire figure. "This. Being calm and measured and serious, as if I'll break if you let me see your joy. I know you're happy. You *should be* happy. Please, please don't force yourself not to be because of me."

And how was she supposed to respond to that? Laugh, shout? Spin in a circle, or insist she didn't want to? How could she be both things—overjoyed and in deep pain—at the same time? Yet she was. So she did the only thing that made any sense given all of that.

She set her bowl down and wrapped her arms around her sister. "I'm sorry, Mahl. I'm sorry this has worked out so well for the rest of us but not for you. I'm sorry you have to make this choice. I want you to be as happy as I am."

Mahlah's arms closed around her too, and her head rested against No'ah. "I want that too. And I have to believe the Lord wants it for me. I just...don't know what will lead me to it. A life with Kapriel? Or is there some other way? Or will He honor whatever I do, so long as I am seeking to honor Him?"

"There are many good paths," No'ah said, as Abba had said so many times through their lives, "that we can walk alongside Him."

Mahlah chuckled—which was good to hear—and gave her a squeeze. "That doesn't help at all. I still want to know what His *best* good is for me."

"I know."

"Mahlah, No'ah. Good morning."

They both started and spun southward, surprised to hear a masculine voice. Men rarely collected the manna for their households—it was the women's job, while the men checked on their animals. But there was Simon, striding toward them, hand lifted.

No'ah returned the greeting along with Mahlah, knowing her confusion was on her face. He wasn't just walking past them, either, on his way to his own tasks. The elder was clearly meaning to halt before them. And the way he focused his gaze on Mahlah said that she had been his whole purpose in coming out so early, into the fields with Manasseh's women.

No'ah stomach sank, and all the joy of Izik's love wasn't enough to overcome it this time. "What has Cozbi said or done *now*?"

Simon's lips twitched into a smile. That was encouraging. A bit. He sent No'ah an amused look but then focused his gaze on Mahlah again. "Your sister cuts right to the heart of the matter, as usual. You've heard the rumors he's been spreading?"

"The lies," Mahlah bit out. She gave one jerk of a nod.

Simon's nod was slower, more thoughtful. "I assumed as much the moment I heard them. I know you too well to think that you'd move from making a hard decision about the young man from the tribe of Benjamin to tossing your affections to Cozbi in a matter of hours." Another twitch of a smile. "For that matter, I can't fathom you tossing your affections to Cozbi at all. Ever."

"She has better taste than that," No'ah couldn't resist saying in agreement.

Simon chuckled. "Izik came to see me yesterday evening too." His gaze flashed to No'ah, a question within it—but he didn't ask. "He said that he and your sister here witnessed the entire exchange that night between you and Cozbi. He stood before the other elders who had come to my tent and gave his testimony. He, furthermore, accused Cozbi of trying to manipulate you into marriage for the sake of your inheritance and begged the tribal elders to examine *his* motivations and hold him accountable for them."

No'ah's heart stuttered, thudded. Her Izik had done that?

Of course he had. He was *Izik*. He couldn't bear to see her sister put in such a situation, no more than he could bear such an obvious injustice. "And? What did the elders say?"

Simon's mirth faded, and he pressed his lips together. "They were torn. Half of us—the ones who know you, Mahlah, and how your father raised you all—believed Izik and voted to caution Cozbi against making any other attempts to force you into a betrothal."

Mahlah swallowed hard. "And the other half?"

Simon's expression twisted with discomfort. "Ours is a big tribe. Everyone knew the Shadow, at least in passing, but not all realized that he'd trained his daughters with weapons. They declared it unreasonable to think that you would go out in the night just for solitude, without a man. Izik *did* have the sense to downplay the fact that the two of you were involved in scaring off those raiders, but your presence outside the camp that night was still not understood. And of course, with Cozbi's grandfather there insisting his grandson has no desire beyond building a family worthy of our tribe and people, and that his upright heart was proven by his confession of his conduct and love for you to his father..." He shook his head. "Some were swayed. They're insisting that you cannot remain unwed, that it is causing too much uproar, and that Cozbi is a reasonable choice."

No'ah reached for Mahlah's hand, and her sister squeezed her fingers so tightly it hurt. No'ah wasn't about to complain.

"I will *not* marry Cozbi," Mahlah ground out from between clenched teeth.

Simon nodded, compassion on his face. "I should hope not. So then...someone else. Choose quickly, my daughter. Before the choice is taken from you."

No'ah squeezed back. It would have to be Kapriel then. On the one hand, she could be happy with that. Kap would be a good husband. They already loved each other, even if the love had been that of siblings. On the other hand, she didn't want her sister to have to *resign* herself to a match with a good man, a good friend. She wanted her to be as happy with her pending future as No'ah was.

Simon moved away, and after a long, silent moment pulsed between them, Mahlah stooped down again and scooped manna quickly into her bowl.

No'ah stared at her for a second, two. How could she just go back to work? How could she keep herself from darting straight back to their tent, or running to intercept Kapriel on the way to or from his morning check on the shepherds and livestock?

How could she keep herself from buzzing this direction and that, whichever way seemed to promise the nectar of answers?

Because Mahlah would be thinking that regardless of what she decided, her sisters still had to eat, and this was their bread. She would be thinking that running out in search of Kapriel wouldn't result in his arriving at their tent, with his parents and Abiram, any faster. Decisions would not be made any better.

She knew her sister's reaction was right. But No'ah's every instinct rebelled against the calm. She couldn't manage the same steadiness and didn't even try. Just went about her half of the chore with buzzing blood and quite a few huffs and stomps as she remembered anew what that snake Cozbi had said. And then a few happy sighs when she thought about Izik, standing tall and firm before the elders. A new grin when she remembered he'd be coming to see her soon.

"That's better," Mahlah said, weak laughter in her voice as they straightened, bowls full, and turned back to their tent. "That's my No'ah."

No'ah stuck her tongue out at her sister and resisted the urge to break into a dance, solely for the sake of the manna in her bowl. She didn't want to take the time to gather it up again.

Each morning chore dragged on and on as it was. The fire took forever to cook the manna cakes, and the trek to the river to bring some extra water in for the day's guests was at least twice as far as it had been yesterday, somehow. Even the birds seemed to be flying by overhead at a lazy half speed, their dives down toward prey or friends slow as a leaf's drift.

By the time Seth's family finally joined them, No'ah felt more like a hive of warring nerves than one cohesive person.

But Izik came in. And his gaze found her in the first second. And he smiled at her in that way that said he knew exactly how she felt, and somehow, somehow he loved her for it, and while it didn't exactly *calm* her, it at least gave her a focus.

She leaped up from the corner Mahlah had exiled her to with a laugh, saying she was ruining everything she was supposed to do after returning with the water, and ran to his side.

His arms were around her. His scent was in her nose. His lips were pressed to her temple. The world was, despite its shadows, a beautiful place.

The rest of the family laughed at their happy reunion, but she didn't mind. She just pressed her cheek to his shoulder and held on until the buzzing receded a bit.

Even with so many of her senses focused on Izik, she still felt it as Mahlah moved through the tent, and she looked up just in time to see her sister's frown. "Where's Kapriel?"

No'ah scanned the collection of people, but sure enough, Izik's brother was nowhere to be seen.

A fact which seemed to surprise his parents. They spun back toward the door, obviously expecting him to be right there.

"He was just behind us," Seth said. He stepped through the flap they'd tied open for the day, looking this way and that.

He must have spotted him, because he halted and relaxed in the way that said his question was answered. Though he didn't come back in.

No'ah shot a question up at Izik. "Was a friend outside?"

Izik shrugged, his smile unapologetic. "I can't say as I paid any attention. I was a bit eager to get inside."

Her returning grin matched his. "What a coincidence. I was a bit eager for you to."

Mahlah held her place in the center of the tent, where she'd stopped when she realized Kapriel hadn't come in yet. Were it No'ah standing there like that, she'd have been fidgeting with her garment and shifting from foot to foot and quite possibly bouncing on her toes. Not Mahlah, of course. She looked completely composed, calm, beautiful.

No'ah glanced at the younger girls, who looked considerably more anxious than Mahlah. That made her feel a *little* better, anyway.

A moment later, Seth came back in, a glance over his shoulder saying he expected Kapriel to be following him.

And he was…but moving far more slowly than usual. And not alone. He had his arm around a figure that was most assuredly female.

Quick anger snapped in her chest. What other woman was he bringing in here? *Now?* Even if someone was injured—which seemed likely, given the way the woman limped into view—did he really think this was the best time to lend aid? Couldn't he have hailed some other cousin to see to her, whoever she was?

The anger sputtered when she saw the woman was old enough to be their mother, silver threaded through her dark hair. Sputtered, but it didn't die. He still could have let someone else help, rather than bringing a stranger into their tent when they were supposed to be planning out his and Mahlah's future.

The breath Mahlah sucked in, though, didn't sound outraged at his audacity. And the hand that flew to her mouth didn't look angry. Just surprised, on both counts. "Gila!"

Gila? No'ah searched her memory for the name, looked long at the woman's face to match it. But she couldn't remember ever seeing her before, and the name meant—no! No'ah sucked in a breath too.

Izik went taut. "Is that…?"

No'ah nodded. "It must be. Uriel's mother."

CHAPTER EIGHTEEN

M ahlah surged forward, wrapping one of her arms around the limping figure of the woman she'd thought, so briefly, she'd someday call Imma. Gila had sprung to her mind several times throughout the night, as all they'd been through, all she had to decide still, swirled through her.

She'd prayed for Gila each time. Prayed that, somehow, the Lord would give her strength. That He would be her sustainer. Prayed that though the Lord had made it clear in multiple ways that Uriel was not the husband He wanted for Mahlah, that Uriel would still return to Him. For his mother's sake, if for no other reason. How would she bear it if she lost her only son to the idols from which she'd fled as a child?

Mahlah's arm brushed Kapriel's as they supported Gila from either side, and she looked over at him, across the woman's bent head. There was no tingle of awareness or excitement at the familiar touch. Even so, there was comfort in knowing that he'd spotted Gila and gone to help her, even given all that passed in the last week.

"Mahlah." Gila's breath was ragged. "Praise God I found you. I didn't know where your tent was, and Manasseh is so *huge*."

"You were looking for me?" She led the woman over to a cushion and helped ease her onto it.

Gila straightened out her bad leg with a wince that spoke of pain well beyond fleeting. She rubbed at her knee. "I only knew that you lived near Kapriel and Izik, and Uriel always said it took him half an hour to walk to their home. But I can't walk as fast as he can—and no one would answer when I asked where your tent was pitched…I was beginning to think I'd never find you. Had I not seen Kapriel—had he not stopped when I called, though he had no reason to…"

Mahlah turned to fetch their guest a cup of water, but Milcah was already moving toward them, filled cup in hand. Hoglah had a plate with a honeyed manna cake on it, and Tirzah settled at Gila's side with a damp cloth in hand. She blotted the sweat from the woman's brow.

Gila blinked rapidly, but it did nothing to hide her tears. "Thank you. You…you are all so gracious."

Mahlah knelt beside Gila's outstretched knee. She didn't know what Uriel had told his mother, but she'd assumed he'd simply cast all the blame on the decision of Moses and stayed mum on her true reasons for rejecting him—his idolatry.

But had he even told her that much? Had he just let her go on thinking a betrothal was still pending?

No. If that were the case, she wouldn't have been surprised at Kapriel's helping her or her sisters' gracious reception. Both things would have been expected, if Mahlah were still planning on marrying Uriel.

So then…what was she doing here?

Gila took a sip of the water, a nibble of the manna, but then set both down beside her with a smile and nod of thanks for her sisters. Mahlah reached for her hand once it was free. "Gila. What's wrong?"

Something had to be. Why else would the woman come hunting for her in the camp of Manasseh, in such a panic that she'd worn herself to near collapse?

Gila opened her mouth but then glanced around at the collection of people and closed it again.

Mahlah looked at her family too, then back to her guest. "My family. These are my sisters, and of course you know Kapriel and Izik, our cousins. That's their father, Seth, one of my father's brothers—and Abiram, the youngest of my uncles. You met Keturah before. His wife but also my imma's sister." She offered what she hoped was an encouraging smile. "You can speak freely with them."

"No." Keturah's word startled Mahlah, but the tone wasn't forbidding. The opposite—understanding. "No, I don't think she'll be comfortable with that. We'll step out for a few minutes. Girls?" She waved a hand to the room at large, and nearly everyone moved toward the door.

Except for Mahlah, of course. And Kapriel, who stepped closer instead, question in his brows, and received a nod of invitation from Gila. No'ah and Izik crowded closer too, her sister's clenched jaw saying she would *not* be dismissed.

Gila didn't know No'ah, but she knew Izik, and she must have put together enough of the relationships to determine that they already knew all there was to know, anyway. She nodded an acceptance of their presence too, but otherwise waited until someone lowered the tent flap, plunging the tent into dimness.

Gila's fingers shook in Mahlah's. "It's Uriel," she said, voice low. "When he told me goodbye this morning, it wasn't his usual quick words to let me know he was tending the animals, with a promise to return by either the midday or evening meal. He said it as though he never means to come back."

Mahlah's breath caught in her throat. What did that mean, exactly? He couldn't intend to do himself harm, could he?

"His cousins." Kapriel whispered the words, his gaze creeping up until it locked on Mahlah's.

Her throat went dry. Were they near, now? The traders who had kept in touch with him all these years? Did he mean to join them?

Gila shook her head, confusion in her eyes. "Gad and Hoshea? I already checked with them, and they said—"

"Not his Benjaminite cousins." Mahlah covered Gila's fingers with her other hand too. "*Your* cousins." At the woman's blank look, she told her what Uriel had explained to them. About how they came regularly, how they'd cut favorable deals with her husband, how they'd told Uriel that they'd never given up the hope of reconciliation with her.

Her blankness moved to horror and then outrage, a river overflowing its banks. She tugged her fingers free of Mahlah's and pressed them to her eyes. "No. No, no, no."

Kapriel lowered from where he'd been standing, into a crouch. "He never told you?"

"Of course he never told me!" Gila's breath shuddered, her hands falling back to her lap. "Because my cousins were not just *traders*. They make and sell idols. Ba'als. If my *husband* did business with them, it wasn't for cloth or spices or herbs. It was for those abominations. Oh." She groaned, doubling over as if she felt sick. "It's no wonder, then. No wonder his flocks never flourished, no wonder my womb closed after Uriel, no wonder that fever took him."

Mahlah didn't know what comfort to offer, especially since she couldn't argue with any of Gila's reasoning. If one of her sisters was in such agony, she would run a hand over their hair, rub their back, hold their hand again. But this wasn't her sister.

Except she was, in a way. She was an adopted daughter of Israel. Family, no matter her blood. Mahlah smoothed back the wisps of hair that had tugged free of Gila's braid and then rubbed what she prayed was a comforting circle on her back. She felt No'ah draw near, and then she was sitting beside Mahlah and adding her own encouraging touch to Gila's back.

After a long moment, the woman drew in a deep breath and sat up. Her eyes were flat. Resigned. Was that what Mahlah had looked like earlier? Maybe, given the look No'ah darted her. If so, then no wonder her sister had been so concerned for her.

"And Uriel?" she asked, voice emotionless. "You think he... he would go to these cousins?"

No'ah glanced to Izik, then Mahlah. "We saw him with a ba'al the other day. Worshiping it."

"That was when I ended things with him," Mahlah added quietly. "What made my decision for me. I'm sorry." Not for cutting things off—she'd had no choice. But she was sorry that this was the truth of Gila's son, her family.

Gila's eyes slid shut. "God, forgive me. I have failed as a mother. All I wanted to do was raise a son who loved You, and… and the one son You've given me has forsaken Your ways."

"You showed Uriel the truth," Kapriel said softly. "That's all any parent can do. It isn't your fault that he chose resentment for those who mistreat you and extended it to the Lord."

"Mistreat me?" Gila's eyes snapped open again. "The people of Israel have been kinder than my own people ever were. Kinder than I expected. Of *course* they were wary of me—how could they not be? But no one ever mistreated me. And if Uriel would say they did, then it is only because he never saw what true mistreatment looks like." She shook her head, tears in her eyes again. "My parents sacrificed three—three!—of my siblings as babies, trying to convince Ba'al to send rain. When that failed, my father blamed my mother and delivered her to the temple to serve as a prostitute—where she was *mistreated* to the point of death. And still our city floundered, and then we heard about the Israelites approaching." Looking fierce now, Gila fisted a hand against her heart. "He would have sent me next. At the age of six. To the temple, to serve the lusts of his friends and neighbors and these *cousins* who claim to miss me. Had he not fallen ill so suddenly and died, I would have too—or lived a life worse than death."

"Have you told him that?" Mahlah asked softly. Surely if she had, Uriel would understand. He would see that however unfair the word of the Lord seemed, it was only meant to keep His people from devolving into such atrocities.

"Of course." Gila's voice dropped. "Years ago. A woman refused to share a meal with me, and he was so angry. So I sat him down and told him everything. Absolutely everything. I thought…I thought he understood."

Mahlah couldn't fathom that he hadn't. That still he'd turned back to the bloodthirsty people she'd escaped. Turned back, worse still, to the god who would ask such things of those who served him.

"If those people are back again, if he thinks to leave with them…" Gila shook her head. "If I had any idea where to find him, I would throw myself at his feet and beg him to change his mind. Pray that this time he would hear me."

Mahlah's stomach twisted. "It's my fault. I pushed him to this when I ended things."

Kap pressed his lips together, though only for a moment. Not long enough to hold in his argument. "You didn't push him anywhere. He had already made his choices, long before you even knew him."

"Kapriel's right." Gila's voice, though, dripped with heartbreak. "If he was going to change for his love of you, then he'd have done it. Your sister never would have seen him worshiping a false god."

She knew that. Her mind did, anyway. But her heart still thumped painfully in her chest, insisting that it couldn't end this way. Gila's only son couldn't just abandon the People she'd chosen and cast his lot with the family that would have sacrificed her.

Mahlah lifted her gaze to Kapriel's. "We need to find him. Talk to him once more. Plead with him."

She expected him to agree with her, like he always did when the matter was one of compassion for their brethren. Instead, his face went hard. Cold. *Hurt.* "You still love him so much?"

That she couldn't stand to see him forsake the only One who mattered? The mother who had all her hopes, all her life pinned on him? Of course she did. She loved *everyone* that much.

Gila sat up straighter. "Would you...would you reconsider? Marrying him? If he swore allegiance to the Lord?"

"No." She didn't have to think about that answer—it was simple fact. Gila's expression drooped, but Kapriel's cleared by the same amount. She offered him a smile too small and tight to really deserve the name, but it was all she could muster. "I'm going to marry Kapriel. And that's part of the reason I want us to try once more to save his friend. Because he'll regret it the rest of his life if he doesn't try."

He would. She knew it. So did Izik and No'ah, given their quick nods. But it took Kapriel a long moment to wrestle that truth into place in his heart. She watched as he did, as he slipped it past his own pain, past what might be best termed jealousy over the thought of her choosing another after all he'd offered her, past the fear that nothing would ever be enough to convince him.

She watched the love of God that He'd told them to hold for their neighbor dislodge each of those things, Kapriel's flickering eyes and shifting expression finally settling into one of peace. He nodded. "He'll be at the glen, I imagine. Perhaps he plans to meet them there, though I can't imagine they'd come in broad daylight."

"Of course they would. They're traders." Izik held out a hand to No'ah, another to Mahlah. "And the traders usually come by midday so they can get back to Shittim or their own camps before nightfall. We don't have much time to lose."

Hope and dread warred over Gila's face. "I want to come— but I'll only slow you down." She patted her knee.

"We'll help you." No'ah held out a hand to her. "And send Kap and Mahlah on ahead."

Gila's nod of agreement was all the permission Mahlah needed. She darted for the door, grabbing up her weapons as she always did, running through the startled collection of family milling along the tents outside and straight for the edge of camp.

Kapriel kept pace with her, pointing southward when she hesitated on the path to the sheepfolds.

They probably should have insisted either Iz or No'ah come with them, to show them the way. "Do you know where we're going?"

Kapriel nodded. "Iz showed me the place, after…after we confronted him. I meant to search for the ba'al and destroy it, but night was falling, and I stopped this side of the stream. I didn't really *want* to see it, truth be told. It was bad enough seeing the place."

She shivered at the very thought. "I can't blame you for that."

They strode a few steps in silence, not quite running but moving far faster than a typical walk. Trying to avoid the notice of all their milling clansmen, though still they had to raise hands in greeting half a dozen times.

Once they'd crossed over into the livestock of Benjamin, Kapriel sent a glance her way. "Did you mean it? That you'll marry me?"

Mahlah nodded. She knew it was the right thing—in her head. But again, her heart hadn't quite caught up yet. Fears still plagued her, and uncertainty and doubt along with them. She just had to trust that the feeling would follow the decision though. That, as Kapriel said, they would build their own fire instead of waiting for lightning. They would stoke it and tend it, and it would warm them for the rest of their lives. That *this* was her best good. "I'll marry you. We'll build a good life together."

He reached for her hand and wove their fingers together. "We will."

She looked out ahead, as if she'd be able to glimpse the future spread before them—then paused, gait hitching and eyes narrowing against the morning sun. She lifted a hand to shield her eyes, focusing on the man driving a few cattle and sheep out of Benjamin's herds. "Is that Uriel?"

Kapriel didn't point out that her recognition, so quick at such a distance, wasn't in fact a good thing. He simply pulled her a few steps farther along, hand shielding his own eyes too, and then muttered something low and sharp. He turned to the nearest shepherd, a boy of perhaps twelve, and motioned to the west. "Where's Uriel going with his animals?"

The boy shrugged, irritation in his every move. "Wouldn't say. Just that he was seeking better pasture, even though we're supposed to stay *here* until the scouts tell us where we should move them next. And he yelled at Lemuel when he said he'd go too."

Better pasture? That didn't bode well. Exchanging a look, they thanked the boy and took off at a jog.

"At least he isn't gone yet," Kapriel said as he ran.

Mahlah was busy looking over her shoulder and waving an arm for No'ah, Iz, and Gila, who had just reached the edge of camp. She hoped they'd be able to see where she and Kapriel were going and not continue to the trees.

Of course, another figure caught her eye too—one she hoped *wouldn't* follow. Cozbi.

At least she knew she could outrun him. "Let's hurry."

They picked up their pace, soon leaving behind the bulk of the flocks and catching up with the tail end of his herd. It was, as Gila had indicated, small. A dozen sheep, three cows. They lumbered along at a half-hearted pace, despite Uriel's continual clucking and calling, as if they knew he meant to lead them away from all their friends and never bring them back again.

It was when he next looked back to make sure the creatures were following that he spotted her and Kapriel. She saw the joy flare, then the sorrow, then the anger. She watched his gaze flick this way and that, seeking an escape that wasn't to be found. His shoulders rolled forward, and his hands curled at his sides.

He locked his gaze on Kapriel, ignoring her entirely. "What are you doing here, Kapriel? Come to gloat? Did you want her for your own all along?"

She wanted to be surprised that he knew she was considering Kapriel for her husband, but she couldn't quite manage it. It had been too logical a step for half the tribe not to have mused about it, and to have passed the musing along to the next tribe over. And though she knew no one had *heard* their conversation at the river last night, countless women had *seen* them.

Kapriel sighed. "No. As I told you when you asked me originally, she was always a sister to me."

Uriel's chin jerked up a notch. "So you aren't going to marry her?"

"I am." He delivered this reply as easily as the previous, palms spread wide. "Because the situation has changed. I'm not going to apologize for it. But that's not why we've sought you out."

"I really don't care why you've come." He stole a quick look at her, seemed to regret it, and spun back to the west. "I'm leaving."

"Please don't." Her voice didn't emerge strong and compelling—it came out in a squeak, broken and cracked.

He paused, half turned. Waited.

She drew in a breath. "Have you considered for even a moment what this will do to your mother? You're all she has."

"She has her *God*." He strode forward again.

"Uriel, wait!" She moved to follow. "Don't you see? You say following Ba'al is easy, but it will take everything from you!"

"I don't have anything left to *take*, Mahlah! You've already done that, you and Moses and Kapriel and your Lord."

He increased his pace, though the animals had begun wandering off the moment he stopped and didn't immediately follow. Maybe he didn't care. Or maybe he'd turn around and gather them again.

She waited a second to see, but he showed no signs of changing course, so she and Kapriel both ran after him again. "Uriel!"

She didn't know what her next argument would be. And she wasn't given the chance to find out. Figures emerged from the trees up ahead—three of them, their shapes and movements eerily familiar. She'd seen them before—just not in the daylight.

Kapriel must have recognized the raiders at the same time. He reached out, grabbed her arm.

Uriel...Uriel lifted a hand. "Uncle! Cousins! Good morning!"

They? *They* were his relatives?

Maybe her eyes were mistaken. It had been dark the other night, after all. They'd never gotten terribly close.

But she knew that lift of the hand—not in greeting but with a bow. She whipped her own off her shoulder, their arrows crossing in flight.

Uriel shouted something. So did Kapriel. So, probably, did she, but it was more noise than words. The strangers were charging in, more missiles flying—a spear, knives, more arrows.

"Stop!" Uriel. "What are you doing? These are my friends!"

Even as he screamed it, another scream came from beside her. *Kapriel.* Mahlah sent the arrow already in her bow and then pivoted, a primal cry ripping from her throat when she saw Kapriel on the ground, a dagger buried to the hilt in his shoulder.

Just the shoulder. Better than the heart or the stomach. Even so. She dropped to her knees beside him, wrapped her hands around the hilt, met his eyes. He nodded. She pulled.

He screamed again and fell backward, but this time she scarcely heard it. Because she glanced down at the dagger in her hands.

And she knew it.

CHAPTER NINETEEN

No'ah pumped her legs as fast as they would go, her hands on the twin sheaths, then her knives in her hand. When she'd seen the figures in the distance emerging from the trees, she'd thought at first that they were just Israelites, heading back to camp from some excursion or another. But then they'd attacked. And their movements were familiar. She'd taken off toward her sister and Kapriel before she could even pause for thought.

Izik started a half beat after her, drew even with her, and soon outpaced her. He shouted, and it might have been something foolish about turning back and seeking safety, but she chose to believe he had more sense than to say something so impossible. She couldn't turn *back* while their siblings needed help. If he was shouting about turning back, it was a shout to the enemy, not to her.

Part of her wanted to glance behind her and make sure Gila hadn't fallen when her two supporters suddenly abandoned her, but the rest of their family had been following in their wake—they'd catch her. No'ah had to focus on what was before her.

She saw the blade strike Kapriel, heard his scream, and then Mahlah's, and then Izik's. She saw her sister follow Kap to the ground, saw her pull out the knife, and knew it must not be a death blow—her sister would have hesitated before removing the blade if it were.

Finally, she was close enough to make out the expression on Mahlah's face—and it went from determined concern to blankness to recognition to rage. As she stood, she looked like some mythical creature rising out of the ashes, ready to tear her enemies to shreds. She held the dagger in her hands as if it were a venomous snake. "Abba!" she screamed.

No'ah faltered, nearly tripped over some invisible obstacle. Why would Mahlah call for their father? She knew well he was beyond coming to her aid.

Then her gaze landed on the dagger—and she understood. No'ah, too, recognized the distinct styling, the colors, the shape of the blade. An exact match of the one that had killed Abba.

As Mahlah spun, she went from holding the blade to gripping it. No'ah reached her side, barely slowing to look down and make sure Kapriel was alive. He was already pushing himself up again. Good.

The three raiders had closed the distance. Perhaps they were out of arrows, because no more of them flew, at least.

Uriel jumped into the space between them, arms spread wide as if he could form a wall through which neither side could break. She couldn't see his face, but his voice rattled with panic as he called out, "Stop! It's Mahlah! They weren't chasing me, not like you think."

The strangers shifted course. So did Mahlah, and No'ah in her wake. Her sister let out a fierce cry, her own dagger in her right hand, theirs in her left. "You! You killed my abba!"

"What?" Uriel spun, arms still out but facing them now, and moved again to block them from each other. "No. You're mistaken. They wouldn't."

"Get out of the way, Uriel," one of the enemy barked. He was an older man, older than any of their parents had been, perhaps as old as Simon. But he was fast, and his arms were corded with muscle, and he held a short, wickedly curved sword as if it were an extension of his arm.

He knew Uriel's name. How did he know Uriel's name? And why would Uriel have offered *Mahlah's* name as if it should bring peace to the situation?

Never mind that. He was getting far too close to Mahlah, and though her sister matched him in height and surely outdid him in rage, knives weren't her strong suit.

They were No'ah's. She skidded to a halt, gave herself half a second to absorb the chaos of their movements and gauge where they'd all go next, and then let her first blade fly. It buried itself in the man's upper arm, just as she'd intended.

He dropped the sword with a scream, and Izik was diving for it, catching it up, rolling back to his feet, and running out of range again before anyone could react.

"Kura, stop." Uriel rushed the now-injured man, blocking him when he tried to lunge for No'ah. "It's only—"

"I heard you the first time." The man—Kura, it seemed—pushed Uriel off him. "She must be killed. She will only call you back here, tie you to these people."

He spat a word she didn't recognize before "people." She could only guess at its meaning—it didn't sound particularly flattering.

"I have no tie on him—I *want* no tie on him, on *any* of you!" Mahlah had shifted her target to another of the men, had made a swipe with the blade, but he'd danced out of range and thrown something at her that she blocked.

"And nothing will bring me back here—there's no reason to hurt each other! She is *nothing*. And, Mahlah, my cousins did not kill your father!"

The third man snarled. "Of course we did."

It was as if all of creation froze, went still. Time stopped. The wind didn't blow. The river stopped flowing. No'ah's heart ceased its beating. She was suspended there, her remaining knife still raised and ready to defend whoever she must, the words physical things that held her immobile.

"For you," the same man continued, shattering the sensation of immobility. "We went to speak with him, as your only relatives. About the girl. He refused us. Said no daughter of his would ever marry a Ba'al worshiper, and then he turned around, as if that was the end of it."

Kura, blood dripping down his arm, scowled. "But she refused you anyway, you said. And here she is, trying to keep you from coming home."

"No. You…" Uriel had been lunging again to put himself between his relatives and hers, but this time when Kura pushed him away, he fell. Hard. And stayed down, as if the ground beneath him couldn't hold him up if he rose. Looking dazed, he turned his head toward them. "I'm…sorry."

The world blurred at the edges. There was movement—more swiping with blades, more jumping out of the way. There were grunts and words and pounding footsteps. Some of them were hers, but she couldn't have said what she did or said or thought. She only knew that these men must either pay the price for Abba's death and pay with their own blood or get so far away from her family that they could never hope to chase them down.

It might have lasted another minute. An hour. She only knew she panted from the effort by the time some new word was spoken in a new voice, and everyone—the three raiders, she and Mahlah, Kapriel and Uriel—went as still as Uriel on the ground.

Gila limped into the space between their lines, her heaving breath saying she'd run to them, despite the protestations of her knee. She didn't lift her arms to form a wall. Didn't throw herself on any of the enemy, as Uriel had tried to do. She had no weapon in her hand. But they fell still. All of them.

"Uncle Kura." Gila spoke the words, the name, as if they were unfamiliar to her lips.

They were, she supposed. How many long years had it been since she'd said them? No'ah watched Kura's arms drift down to his sides. He moved a few steps closer. "Gila."

She turned her head to take in the other men too. Her cousins? Given their ages, it seemed likely. Kura's sons, or perhaps a grandson. The youngest of the men looked near No'ah's age.

"What are you doing here? I told you decades ago that I was where I wanted to be."

"You were a child. You didn't know." Kura sliced his injured arm through the air. "And then they cast a spell on you. But you are *ours*, Gila. Your son is ours. These destroyers, these people who turned our homes to rubble and murdered our families—they don't get to keep you."

Gila shook her head. "Our *homes* were scars on the land that took and used and never gave back. Our *families* were murderers themselves, generations of them—a blight that refused to accept healing. The greatest mercy of my life was when they took me in and allowed me to become one of them. I'm an Israelite now, Uncle. Not yours. And neither is my son."

Shadows flickered and danced over Kura's face, in his eyes, onto his lips. A thousand angry hornets darting and buzzing, ready to sting. "He says otherwise."

Gila looked over to Uriel. He was standing again, staring back, eyes so very empty. "Don't leave, my son," she bade, voice far calmer than it had been in their tent.

Uriel swallowed. "I...don't know how to stay. I don't—they killed him. Because of *me*. Because I..."

"They made the choice," Mahlah said, hands still gripping her weapons with white knuckles. "Not you. You can come back from this, Uriel. Put aside the idols. Repent. The Lord will forgive you."

His face twisted in agony. "But will you?"

"Yes."

No'ah didn't know how her sister could deliver the word so calmly, with such surety. But even No'ah, who knew her better than anyone, believed she meant it. Which made resentment buzz in her chest. How could she offer forgiveness so easily? It was Uriel's very affection for her that had led to Abba's death!

That wasn't something to be set aside. It wasn't something to be understood.

It wasn't something to be forgiven.

And yet...it was no sin to love her sister. How could he, how could anyone, not? For all his faults, all his sins, the great infidelity that only the Lord could wipe clean, he'd done no wrong in his pursuit of Mahlah. Even telling his family about her was a good and honorable thing, despite them not being of Israel.

He couldn't have known what they would do—either in approaching Abba or killing him.

Mahlah was right. The sin was theirs, not his. The price theirs to pay.

She shifted, not really knowing why until she blinked the greater world back into focus and realized she'd been responding to Izik's movements, Kapriel's. They'd been shifting slowly to be behind the three Amorites, and she'd moved with them, closing them in while the rest of her family approached from the camp with more caution.

The strangers must have become aware of it at the same moment, their distraction with Gila done. Kura cursed, spun in a circle, spat. From his belt, he took another knife, holding it in his blood-stained hand. "You are an abomination to your people, Gila. Your leaving put a curse on us all. If you will not come back with us, then your blood will have to appease Ba'al."

He lunged. No'ah lunged after him. Kapriel and Izik and Mahlah all moved to intercept the other two.

But Uriel moved first and fastest. With "No!" screaming from his lips, he jumped between his uncle and his mother, arms spread wide like a wall.

Kura had already leaped. His blade already swooped down. By the time No'ah landed on him with her own blades, the damage had already been done. Uriel sagged to the ground, all life extinguished from his eyes.

⸻

Mahlah dabbed a bit more precious honey on Kapriel's shoulder, tossing the blood-soaked rag she'd used to clean his wound into the little eddy of water and rocks. The rocks would hold it there, but the river water would wash most of the grime and blood from it before she even bent down to scrub it out.

The wound was long and curved, matching the profile of the blade. Healing would take longer than a straight blade's wound would have—but he was alive. Praise the Lord for that.

He sat on a wide, flat rock at the river's edge, his tunic tied at the waist so she had access to the full scope of his injury. They weren't near where all the women would be coming for their water, but they were still within sight of camp.

Not that anyone would say anything about her being with him now, tending his wound instead of letting his mother do it. She was his betrothed, as of an hour ago. They would be married within the week.

"I'm sorry."

Mahlah looked up at his soft words, into his eyes. "For what?" If he'd been reading her mind while she tended him, he could be apologizing for how quickly the betrothal happened— but that had been her choice as much as his. When Cozbi had arrived at the site of the small battle, had seized upon the ba'al that had fallen from Uriel's bag at some point, had tried to say it was Kapriel's...well. *None* of the elders had believed that for a second, even before Gila had thrown herself on their mercy and confessed that it was her son's, bought from the uncle and cousins she had disowned forty years before. Even so, Cozbi's schemes would only get worse, more dangerous.

So she'd taken Kapriel's hand, they'd strode up to Simon, and they'd announced before anyone near enough to hear them—which seemed like a quarter of the tribe of Manasseh and half of Benjamin besides—that they would marry.

Kapriel held her gaze, and it felt as if he held her hand again instead. "You lost the man you loved today."

Mahlah sighed and set the little pot of honey down carefully on the rock. "No, I didn't." She picked up his hand and held it between hers. Looked *him* in the eye.

He frowned. "I know you cared for him."

She nodded. "I did. Perhaps he was my bolt of lightning. But you were thinking in the right direction yesterday, I think, Kap. The love isn't the lightning—that's just attraction, excitement. The love is in the fire it kindles. But there can be lightning without fire—and fire without lightning." She leaned closer, into the space they usually kept open between them by some unspoken agreement. She watched him notice, his eyes flicker, saw him swallow.

They'd never stopped to consider attraction before. They'd never sought it. But it could be there, now that they were looking. It could grow, and it would be easy enough to let it. "I'm choosing the fire we build. With you. Because the fear that flooded me when you were hit, when you were down—that far outweighed the sorrow of Uriel. I regret that he died, and how. But had *you* died..." She shook her head. "I barely knew him. But you're my whole life."

They leaned in together, slowly and deliberately, a million unspoken things flying between them, using their locked gazes as a path. He was afraid too, as she was. He was reeling too, from all that happened so quickly. But both of them would rather sing life's song, dance life's dance, flow onward in life's river, than risk losing all that mattered.

Their kiss was a gentle thing, a soft promise. At first. Then she shifted a little, and so did he, and somehow, a spark flared up. Fanned bright. Caught hold.

When she pulled away eventually, she couldn't help but laugh. "Well then. Fears assuaged."

His eyes sparkled to match his smile. "Guess we could have tried that yesterday and saved ourselves a sleepless night." He patted the rock beside him.

She slid into her place beside his good arm so that he could slip it around her. "There is one thing though."

"Hmm?" His face turned to hers, their eyes on a level.

Her fingers moved as they would over her harp, the melody pairing with words that spoke of hope. "I'd like…I'd like to adopt an imma."

It only took him a beat. "I don't think it works quite that way," he said. But amusement laced his tone.

She shrugged. "Perhaps not legally. But she has no one else. Where will she go when the land is divided? And she has so few friends. Plus—"

"Mahlah." He leaned over, pressing another soft, gentle kiss to her lips. "Gila can live out the rest of her days with us, if she agrees."

"Really?" She hadn't thought he'd refuse…she just hadn't dared assume he'd agree. "You don't mind?"

"That your heart is as big as the Promised Land?" He smiled and pulled her closer. "I don't mind that at all."

CHAPTER TWENTY

The land spread before them, a dazzling rainbow of greens deeper than No'ah had ever seen, blues richer than she'd thought possible, of reds and oranges and yellow dappling the meadows and trees with food enough for them all.

Grains waved in the fields, nearing harvest. Rivers and brooks gurgled with life. Vines sagged with grapes.

She could see for miles from this vantage point, and she might have gone running down the hill, laughing with abandon, had the very thought not made her feet ache and the weight in her stomach stretch a protest. She rubbed a hand over the little life inside her and promised the baby she'd be patient. For now, anyway.

Izik rubbed at the spot in her back that always hurt after a few hours of walking, scanning the land before them just as she was doing. "What do you think? That side...or this one?" He motioned to the east, to the west. All land that belonged to their family. Dividing it up further, among all the inheriting brothers—and sisters—had been left to the elders.

Which, naturally, meant they'd all be making their voices heard.

"Hmm." She leaned into his side, studying the landscape. "I do like being near the river...but then, those vineyards make for a fine vista. Or—up with those fruit trees there. That could be perfect."

"You can have them." Mahlah came up on her other side, a hand on her own swollen abdomen—though her babe wasn't due to come for *months* after No'ah's. "You'll be climbing them anyway, the moment you've put your babe down for his first nap."

No'ah chuckled at the thought. "You do have a point." She looked over her shoulder, searching for their other sisters in the crowd of cousins and aunts and uncles surging up the road toward their new home. She found each of them with their husbands, laughing and pointing at this or that, making their own plans. Gila strode in the midst of them, keeping up without trouble now that her injured knee had mended. Her smile was the sort of bright that spoke of peace, of homecoming. The sort all the brighter for the shadows underscoring it.

She'd never get her son back. But she had daughters now. Five of them.

"It's so beautiful." Kapriel, at Mahlah's side, of course, sighed a happy sigh. "I still can't believe half the tribe stayed behind. Gave up their claim to this."

No'ah didn't either, even having seen how lovely the land was that they'd claimed on the other side of the Jordan. It wasn't *this*. Wasn't the Promised Land. "I can't say as I'm sorry—given that Cozbi was part of that half."

Mahlah snorted her agreement. He'd admitted defeat once she and Kapriel were betrothed and then married quickly thereafter, yes. But he hadn't been gracious about it. If he'd been their permanent neighbor, they'd be constantly looking over their shoulders, waiting for their livestock to "wander" into his folds or something to "accidentally" spoil their grain.

Izik started them down the hill. "Asher said there are a few houses already built on the parcel."

"Those will have to go to the elders though, of course," Kapriel said. "We'll plan on building. It shouldn't take long to raise each one, if we're all working together."

No'ah's lips twitched. They acted and spoke as if they knew all there was to know about building houses, just because they'd put tents up and down all their lives. She had a feeling there would be a few tricks they had to learn in the doing. But then, they'd just keep on living in the tents until that day. It wasn't as though they knew anything else anyway.

She tucked her hand into Izik's and walked beside her sister down the road. Their road, to their land. Something no Israelite had ever been able to claim before. For the first time since Abraham left Ur, they were *home*. A place to call their own.

She didn't realize she was humming until Mahlah picked up her line. Until her other sisters joined in behind her. She didn't realize *what* she was humming until they all sang the words together.

Abba's favorite hymn of praise. The Shadow's Song, as the people now called it. No'ah smiled as she sang. Her abba's body was buried on the plains outside Shittim, in a place she'd never go again.

But he was here with them. Among his brothers. Through his daughters. He lived on in the praises he'd taught them. In the lives they lived. In the land before them.

He was here—and he sang with them as they marched into their land.

Letter from
THE AUTHOR

Dear Reader,

The last time I read the Bible chronologically in a year, these five daughters mentioned in both Numbers and Joshua really stood out to me. What must it have been like, to be the sole female inheritors among all the brethren of Israel? Clearly they were unmarried when they petitioned...but then Moses says they should *marry whomever they wish,* so long as it was within their tribe. The decision was put firmly in their hands—they were given footing equal, in some ways, with men. We aren't told their thoughts on the matter or whether marrying their cousins felt like "settling," just that they all married sons of their father's brothers and then claimed their portion for their father.

In my mind, though, the very need for that revision begs the question of *why?* Why would the elders have brought the concern before Moses unless one of the sisters had made them think it necessary? Pure speculation on my part, of course, but one that I hope you found enjoyable!

Much of my character-building in this one is based on the meaning of each character's name. *Zelophehad* means "the shadow or tingle of fear," so I crafted him as a man who would inspire that in others. *Mahlah* means "harp," *No'ah* means "motion," *Hoglah* means "dance," *Milcah* means "queen," and *Tirzah* means "delight." I loved how, taken together, their names paint a picture of a joyful, regal performance, full of energy. I decided that would be what won them the favor of Moses even before they asked him their question. I did take some liberties with the conversations with Moses, adding some personal commentary from him and making their petition have more of an explanation in it. Though these parts are fiction, they still preserve the heart of the recorded dialogue.

Finally, I wanted to touch on the most dangerous form of unfaithfulness in this story, which comes on the heels of a plague that wiped out those who took pagan wives: unfaithfulness to God. Idolatry was a constant threat to true worship of the Lord, and we'd be naive to think it stopped when setting up wooden idols in our homes went out of fashion. Every time I read about idol worship, I pause to ask myself, "What am I putting before the Lord? What do I set up around me that I then work for, think of most, or love more than Him?" The heart of humanity has never changed—neither its weaknesses nor its virtues.

May we never forget to keep our eyes always on Him…and may He fill our mouths with song and our feet with the joy of worship.

Roseanna

BOOK GROUP QUESTIONS

1. Had you noted the story of the daughters of Zelophehad before when you read Leviticus? What struck you about their story?

2. Each of the sisters has her own special gift and place in the family. Which one do you relate to most? Have you noticed similar complementary gifts in your own family?

3. The meaning of each character's name plays a key role in their personality in this story. Do you know what your name means? Does it influence you at all?

4. The sisters were part of the generation that got to move into the Promised Land, the first time the Israelites had ever claimed land as their own. How do you think you would have felt in their situation? What surprises do you think lay in store for them?

5. Repeatedly throughout their history after the Exodus, Israel was purged of idolators. Why do you think faithlessness to the Lord persisted even after these shows of power? Have you ever tried to understand those who were punished, to see the Lord through their eyes?

6. Moses is a well-known figure in the Bible, of course, but given the size of Israel, many of them would never have met him personally. What did you think of the sisters'

reactions to meeting him? How would you have felt in their situations?

7. Had you been in Mahlah's situation, how would you have reacted to Moses's second decree about who she must marry?

8. Do you believe that romantic love is something that strikes you, like lightning, a fire that you can choose to build and tend, or a combination of the two?

9. Who was your favorite character? Why?

10. What was your favorite part of the story? Did anything in it help you view the biblical history of entering the Promised Land in a new way?

A SCHOLAR'S VIEW OF BAAL

Let's go back to the days of Mahlah and No'ah. We are in a prescientific era with only the movements of the sun and the moon to guide us. We fear that spirits inhabit the streams and lakes, with magical forces everywhere that can cause us great harm if we do not appease them. With the threat of snowstorms, we must huddle around a fire with animal skins covering our bodies. It's not easy to survive!

Everyone knows that the crops must come again in the spring and the animals must reproduce if we are to keep food on the table. Other than the mechanics of reproduction, we know nothing about how there will be enough provision to continue to meet our needs. Is there an answer? People around us say that we need to worship Baal.

But what in the world is Baal?

Baal is the title given to the god worshiped by the Canaanites and Phoenicians. The son of their chief god, El, Baal was a god of fertility. This was all new to the Hebrews. Baal often took the form of a ram or a bull, referencing fertility. While the Jewish people survived the desert by the hand of Jehovah, some began to fear that their god of war might not be up to working as a god of agriculture.

Archeological excavations have dated this form of paganism as far back as 2000 BC. Documentation indicates that Baalism swept across Egypt in 1400 BC, but it existed long before this time. A hallmark of Baal worship was sacrificing pigs and eating pork. Subsequently, the Israelites were forbidden to eat pork, and they keep the rule to this day.

Israelites turned their attention toward this god who was said to have the ability to make the crops grow and the cattle expand the herd. The worship of Baal penetrated Jewish religious life early in the period of the Judges. During the disastrous reign of King Ahab, Baalism became common. Hezekiah's son rebuilt the shrines of Baal and the Canaanite goddess Asherah that Hezekiah had destroyed. When Scripture mentions "the high places," the references are to temples used to worship Baal and seek his blessing on the land and the animals.

Another option was Baal-peor, a god of the Moabites. Terrible rites occurred on a high place called Mount Peor. The observances of the Moabites became another temptation to Israel. The Israelites might argue that since the Moabites were their distant cousins, what could be wrong with their god Baal-peor? It took an upheaval to open their eyes.

When the prophet Elijah challenged the prophets of Baal on Mount Carmel (I Kings 18), he proposed a confrontation between Baal and Yahweh. The 450 prophets of Baal did everything they could to get their god to act. After nothing happened, Elijah built his altar with twelve stones to represent the tribes and then drenched the altar with water. When he called on the Lord, fire from heaven consumed the wood and wet sacrifices. The people fell on their faces to worship the true God, and the 450 false prophets were slain. The truth had been revealed.

In Scripture, Baalism has always been condemned in no uncertain terms. In a list of transgressions, Baalism is there right along with other crimes. Jeremiah asked, "Will you steal, murder, commit adultery, swear falsely, offer sacrifices to Baal, and follow other gods that you have not known...?" (Jeremiah 7:9)

Through the centuries we can observe Baalism evolving into other forms. The need for fertility and reproduction didn't change, but the gods took on new names and forms depending on what part of the world one lived in.

Where do we find our security today? Our hopes fulfilled? Our dreams obtained? Might Baalism have come again?

We may go to church on Sunday, but sometimes our attention focuses on Monday morning and our job, which is how we make money to live. Our security resides in rockets, missiles, and the military, not in those prayers offered up during Sunday worship. Of course, there's nothing wrong with earning a living or being protected by the military and their armaments. However, when we make these things our source of hope, then we've got a *big* problem.

Whatever gives us ultimate meaning and purpose is by definition our god. Husband or wife, investments or wealth, status or achievement, power and control, on and on. When these entities compete with the Lord God Almighty in our hearts, the struggle is called idolatry.

In the present, as in the past, we find the same message from God to His people. We must give absolute fidelity to Him. He and He alone is our security.

How did this affect Mahlah and No'ah's experience? The daughters of Zelophehad were concerned for their inheritance but wanted to follow the law. They wanted to stay on the side of righteousness. Neither the Talmud nor the Zohar tell us what is meant when the daughters said the father "died in his own sin." The deed may have been no more serious than gathering sticks on the Sabbath. Rabbinic sources believed the daughters were wise and righteous students of the Torah. They argued for their inheritance by making analogy to the law and were equally faithful by marrying men of their tribe.

The larger issue was a concern for loss of land that was to go to the tribe of Manasseh. If the daughters inherited the land and then married men outside their tribe, at their death the land would go to the other tribe. By agreeing to marry *within* their tribe, the matter was settled.

Exploring the past has taught us how important it is to worship the one true God alone as our sustainer. His law is still to be followed regardless of any other circumstance. It is an unchanging truth that if we put our trust and hope in Him, He will always sustain us.

Fiction Author
ROSEANNA M. WHITE

———————————

Roseanna M. White is a bestselling, Christy Award–winning author who has long claimed that words are the air she breathes. When not writing fiction, she's homeschooling her two kids, editing, designing book covers, and pretending her house will clean itself. Roseanna is the author of a slew of historical novels that span several continents and thousands of years. Spies and war and mayhem always seem to find their way into her books... to offset her real life, which is blessedly ordinary.

Nonfiction Author
ROBERT L. WISE, PH.D.

———————————

The Rev. Robert L. Wise, Ph.D., is the author of thirty-five books and numerous articles published in English, Spanish, Dutch, Chinese, Japanese, and German. On the internet he weekly publishes *Miracles Never Cease* and monthly presents live interviews on YouTube with people who have experienced divine interventions.

Read on for a sneak peek of another exciting story in the
Extraordinary Women of the Bible series!

DAYS OF AWE: EUODIA & SYNTYCHE'S STORY

BY TEXIE SUSAN GREGORY

April 60 AD

Deep, guttural sobs grated the room's air. Euodia knelt by the burly man's pallet and placed a hand on his sweat-drenched forehead to soothe him.

"Hush, Rafe. All is well. You're safe. Safe and healing."

"Not Rafe. Cerberus." His voice bore the hoarseness of disuse.

She sat back on her heels and frowned, uncertain—no, hoping—she'd misunderstood. "Cerberus, the *kunun*?"

He grunted once. Cerberus. The unofficial hound of Christ followers who, like his name, was a hunter, tracking down believers to harass and oppress. The man who ten years ago dragged Paul before the magistrates after he freed a slave from an evil spirit.

Cerberus opened one swollen eye and glared at her. She averted her gaze but refused to surrender to instinct and skitter backward. If he suspected she was a Christ follower, he'd shun her help and drag himself back to the alley where Brother Clement found him bleeding from knife wounds.

The flat-footed slap of bare feet alerted Euodia to her sister's approach. She stood abruptly, placing herself between the entrance and Cerberus's face to block his view. He must not see Syntyche. Her fearless, determined sister would so offend him by proclaiming Jesus as God that she'd be arrested for being a nuisance.

"Dear one." She'd not use her sister's name and further endanger her. "Please, come with me into the courtyard. I must tell you who..."

Syntyche brushed past her. "You are Cerberus. I am Syntyche." She paused. "A Christ follower."

Euodia's shoulders slumped.

His battered face tightened, curling the split lip into a bloody snarl. Euodia tugged at her sister's arm. Syntyche jerked free.

"Leave us." She motioned toward the door. "Brother Clement is waiting outside."

Euodia reached the door before realizing she'd once again obeyed her sister without question. She turned back, hesitant to leave her sister alone with Cerberus. He was a threat, even badly beaten and wounded.

Syntyche knew her well. She'd turned as if waiting to shoo her out the door. A flick of Syntyche's wrist, and Euodia scurried away. Lingering would earn her a sharp reproof.

Clement stood when she entered the atrium.

Questions rose and toppled, jumbling for first utterance until all she managed was, "I don't understand."

He nodded. "Brother Syzygus is a man I respect. Together we chose to withhold the patient's name, thinking you'd be more comfortable not knowing who you healed. Two weeks is a long time to be anxious in someone's presence even if he was unconscious much of that time."

"So, you knew his name from the beginning, and you told my sister. You trusted her with his name but not me."

"I did. Forgive me, please." Despite his words, he did not appear contrite. "It was to ease your way, but it was wrong. You said he'd be here another week. Will knowing who you serve make this task more difficult? Someone can guard you while you tend to him."

Euodia folded her arms across her chest, unwilling to be placated. "And you brought him into your home, and he knows our names."

"Not yours."

"You have put us all at risk with your decision. Even your *mater.*"

Clement ran a hand over his lightly graying beard. "Sister Euodia, I have learned the hard way to do nothing without seeking the Lord's guidance first. I was led down an alley I never walk and found a man I never wanted to meet—much less help. This is not my doing. Look for the Lord's hand in this and wait with great expectation for what He will do."

Euodia crossed the room to a padded bench and sank into its softness. Leaning her head against the frescoed wall, she counted and recounted the red, yellow, and blue circles ornamenting the ceiling. After a few minutes, she lifted her head and pinned him with her gaze.

"My sister is alone with our greatest oppressor. What do you think she can do?"

Clement raised an eyebrow. "Is there anything your sister can't do when the Lord guides her?"

His words stung. Even the church leaders believed Syntyche to be always capable, always confident, always perfect.

Syntyche studied the man before her, then bowed her head asking for guidance. Looking at him again, she saw beneath the battered face covered with stubbled beard, past the Roman-styled hair, beyond the tense lips, to a child—an angry, confused little boy.

"Cerberus, I'm going to tell you a story. You can listen or sleep or interrupt, but I will not stop speaking."

He neither acquiesced nor objected. She'd not expected a response.

"You and I may live as Romans, but we are Greek—from name to nose. We know the stories of our ancestors and the gods of our people. Like you, I have offered incense and votives at the temples, sung hymns, and celebrated the festivals." She leaned closer. "This is what I learned. We must go to our gods and do and give and beg and bribe them for favor and grovel to avoid their wrath. It is the way of life, yes?"

Cerberus gave an infinitesimal nod.

"There is another way, a God who came to love us—Jesus, the Savior."

His cheeks drew inward, his jaw worked and spit hurled forth. Syntyche wiped it from her face. It was not the first time she'd been spat upon. Her people believed spitting thwarted an evil presence.

"As Greeks, we worship many gods. Our loyalty is divided, and we cannot keep each one content. Grace does not exist. With the Christ, there is no guilt, no wrath, no condemnation. Let me tell you how this came to be and how it has changed my life.

"Darkness covered the souls of all people. Fathomless darkness so deep no light could penetrate. Yet something dwelled within each person, an inexplicable desire they could grasp only a sliver of—a yearning for light."

She knew he was hearing the story she told. At times his hands twitched, or his body shifted. His shoulders would tense, and then his very stillness assured her he listened.

She finished and withdrew without a farewell. Lingering in the atrium, she walked beside the pool of water, needing a moment alone before joining Clement, his mater, Helena, and Euodia in the gardens where they'd been praying for her witness. Tomorrow and every day Cerberus remained under Clement's roof, she'd share a bit more—her story, Saul's transformation to Paul, Jesus's harder teachings.

Syntyche traced a blue swirl on one of the columns. She'd always been bold, making a choice and advancing undeterred. Faith was harder, waiting to be shown His way, allowing only His words to pass her lips. It frightened her—this vulnerability—this walking blindly with the Lord and only Him. Since her husband's death five years ago…

"Syntyche!"

She blushed when Clement spoke her name, and again upon realizing Euodia's eyes had lit with mischief. If her little sister said anything to Clement or Helena, she'd…

Euodia crossed the room and touched her elbow. "Did he hear you, Sister?"

"How could he not? I'm not known for being soft-spoken." She laughed then sobered. "The question is, did he hear the Lord?"

Euodia pulled back. "Of course, that's what I meant." She glanced up at the light flowing through the roof opening. "Forgive me, but I need to return home. My husband will wonder where I am. You will return tomorrow?"

"As long as I have a captive audience, he will hear my witness. If he turns away from the Lord, it will not be from ignorance. Euodia, how much longer before he is well enough to be moved?"

Clement answered for her. "His family returned from their travels early. They sent word they are hiring physicians and preparing a room for him. Mater spoke with them and insisted he was not ready to travel, but his wife was adamant he'd be better off with them. A covered litter will arrive for him in three days."

Syntyche grinned. "Three days? An auspicious number for Cerberus to be spiritually dead and then receive eternal life, Lord willing."

The next day, Euodia rubbed her sweaty palms against her clothes and tried to still the fluttering in her stomach before opening the door to Cerberus's cubicle. Knowing who she was serving bothered her more than she wanted to admit. It was not the giving of her time and skills that concerned her, it was fear of reprisal—of the humiliation of being whipped and the subsequent pain that lingered for weeks. She'd tended believers who'd been flogged and seen the agony as she mended their torn flesh. Cerberus was known throughout Philippi as a cunning hunter whose prey suffered when they were caught.

Legs trembling, she forced herself to approach his pallet and kneel beside him as she'd done each day for over two weeks. She swallowed, pulled at the neck of her clothes. Was the room always so warm?

This time, there was no grunt of acknowledgment or raised hand to greet her. She loosened the bandages to reapply honey on the wounds she'd stitched. He did not flinch. She probed the swelling in his arm. He said nothing. He did not blink when she soothed salve over the cuts on his face.

"Are you in pain?" She examined the gashes, but no red streaks of infection radiated from the wounds. "Are you thirsty? Hungry? Chilled?"

No answer. Perhaps he was embarrassed a woman was tending him. Or maybe he was miffed she'd referred to him as a kunun, a vicious dog. She'd assumed he'd be proud of the epithet, since his was the name of the multiheaded dog who guarded Hades preventing the dead from escape.

Her work complete, she gathered pouches of herbs and ointment jars and returned them to her medical box. Silently, she studied him.

Yesterday, had her sister so offended him with her witness that he refused to speak? She shrugged. Syntyche would return to share the story of their Lord. If Cerberus was annoyed about hearing it once, he'd soon be livid.

"Syntyche will return today."

The pulse in his neck quickened.

"She will not be deterred. Our Lord means everything to her—to us—and she will tell you about Him no matter what you do to her later. She knows the danger she faces by speaking to you."

He said not a word. It was as if she did not exist, had not spoken, had not been heard.

Syntyche shivered in the morning chill. Again today, she'd speak of salvation and the Anointed One, the Savior, to Euodia's patient. Yesterday, Cerberus's barely suppressed rage had not frightened her. Fury meant something touched an ache deep inside him.

She'd been angry when told she needed a savior. How dare anyone suggest she could not please the gods on her own strength? No one tried harder than she had to excel, until, disheartened and disenchanted, she no longer desired to please anyone or anything. The Christ was different, offering salvation and hope when tragedy splintered her life.

Helena's handmaid opened the door when Syntyche reached Clement's house. The scent of quince—apples and oranges and vanilla—wafted through the house. These gently warming months with their earthy fragrance were her favorite time of year.

She slipped off her sandals and paused a moment by the smoldering brazier to pray.

Lord, guide my every word.

Cerberus lay propped against a pile of pillows. Seeing her, he immediately turned his head to the wall and closed his eyes. As the swelling in his face had lessened, she could see his jaw tighten.

If he thought ignoring her would offend or stop her from speaking, he would soon realize his mistake. Nothing stopped God's gift from being shared.

She sat an arm's length from his side and began.

"Darkness covered the souls of all people. Fathomless darkness…" She repeated each word of the story, and even though he did not watch her, she knew the joy and sorrow of the story showed on her face and burst through her voice.

"Then the Creator of all—the Creator of mercy and grace—heard the cries of desperation." She choked, remembering her own darkness and desperation. "He became an infant, a helpless one, as we were helpless."

She felt Him speaking through her, her own voice familiar to her but the words not her own. She was a channel, an aqueduct of His message to this man.

The story complete, she rose and without another word, left the room.

Staring into the atrium's pool, she wondered if the seeds of Christ had taken root. In a moment of fear, she wrapped her arms around herself. Would Cerberus be saved, or she killed?

Rose perfume reached her before Helena called a greeting. "Syntyche, come and break your fast with me. I have food laid out for us in the alcove."

The two women gathered around a meal of cheese, grapes, freshly squeezed juice, and *mekici*. The flat, doughy cakes, fried until they were a light gold, oozed with creamy yogurt. Syntyche licked her lips, savoring the treat.

"The best part, Helena, is that someone else made them."

"If you weren't known to be such a good cook, others wouldn't be afraid to prepare food for you. I dared not tell my cook that Syntyche would be eating these. She'd have gone to bed insisting her head was throbbing and we'd have not seen her until you left."

Syntyche reached across the table and caught Helena's blue-veined hand between hers. "Tell me the truth. Am I that frightening?"

"Yes, dear, you are." Helena squeezed the younger woman's hands. "No, now do not pull away. Listen to me. You are fearless in speaking of our Lord. That shames those of us who are not as bold—especially the men. You are the most excellent cook in Philippi—better than anyone twice your age." She cocked her head. "How *do* you know exactly which seasonings are best and what amount to use? You are young enough to remarry. That unnerves the younger women."

"I do not mean to—"

"These are all good things. Our Lord has given you many gifts to use for Him. Do not hesitate or fear to do so."

"Sometimes I fear, Helena." She whispered as if afraid to hear her own words. "I fear speaking out for our Lord will lead to my death and there will not be time to say goodbye to those I love."

Helena reached over and lifted Syntyche's chin. "Then you must love them well each day."

"Today is our farewell." Euodia massaged the lightly scabbed wounds framing Cerberus's face. "The swelling is down, and your color is better. Keep honey on the gashes I stitched."

"Traitor."

His growled insult was loud. Good, he was gathering strength.

She held her breath against his stench and moved closer to clean the last trace of pus from a slash beneath his arm. He'd refused her attempts to bathe him since regaining consciousness.

Euodia chuckled to herself. When he was well enough to return to the baths, all the water would need to be replaced, soiled from his weeks-long sweat.

"I'm not a traitor. I'm a loyal citizen." She held up a hand. "Save your breath. I'm not an atheist either, as you've repeatedly accused me. I worship a different God than you."

"You believe what your sister says?"

"Not a word of it." Enjoying the shock in his eyes, she waited a moment before continuing. "Not because she said it. I believe what the Lord has revealed to me, what I've heard read from the Hebrew scriptures, and what Paul taught us of the Anointed One."

"Paul." He snorted.

"Tomorrow you return to your family." She bit her tongue, refusing to beg for leniency when eventually he'd order her and her sister to be arrested. Her sister might brave the prisons, but Syntyche never feared anything. Not trusting herself to do more than nod farewell, she stood, gathered her healing supplies, and left the room.

Blowing a kiss to Helena, she hurried outside and inhaled the air's freshness. She hoped to be home before her husband knew how long she'd been away. He knew she was a Christ follower but not how much time she spent among the believers. Shaking off a twinge of guilt, she walked faster. Besides, Marcellus had spent the morning attending an interview, and she wanted to know how he felt about it.

* * *

Syntyche brushed the street dust from her clothes and watched Euodia scurry away. As much time as her sister had invested in the patient, had she even once seized the opportunity to speak of the Lord? She loved her little sister, but Euodia needed to be less concerned with what others thought of her and more outspoken for the Lord.

She pushed open the door to Cerberus's room. Propped against a pile of pillows, he stared at the far wall. She strode forward to stand at the foot of his pallet.

"Cerberus, I have a request."

He shifted his gaze to her, his face unwelcoming, his eyes shuttered.

"When you are well—and I pray you will heal completely— arrest me if you must, but spare Euodia and Brother Clement. Euodia has done nothing but try to help you, and Clement rescued you from the rats and scavengers of the back alley. You owe your life to both of them."

Syntyche waited for a nod, an indication he'd honor her request or at least consider it. Neither a flicker in his eyes nor a subtle motion of his head betrayed his thoughts.

"Very well. I will not stay today, but know this—our prayers for you will not stop when you return home. They will not stop no matter who you arrest nor how you treat us."

She pivoted and closed the door behind her. She'd spoken to Cerberus as the Lord instructed and stopped when His words left her mind. There were others who needed to know about the Savior. She listed them in her mind: her brother, the women she worked with, strangers in the marketplace. With each step she searched for the next person she'd be guided toward to witness to about Him—so many to speak with before her arrest.

A Note from
THE EDITORS

W̲e hope you enjoyed another exciting volume in the Extraordinary Women of the Bible series, published by Guideposts. For over seventy-five years, Guideposts, a non-profit organization, has been driven by a vision of a world filled with hope. We aspire to be the voice of a trusted friend, a friend who makes you feel more hopeful and connected.

By making a purchase from Guideposts, you join our community in touching millions of lives, inspiring them to believe that all things are possible through faith, hope, and prayer. Your continued support allows us to provide uplifting resources to those in need. Whether through our communities, websites, apps, or publications, we inspire our audiences, bring them together, and comfort, uplift, entertain, and guide them. Visit us at guideposts.org to learn more.

We would love to hear from you. Write us at Guideposts, P.O. Box 5815, Harlan, Iowa 51593 or call us at (800) 932-2145. Did you love *The Shadow's Song: Mahlah and No'ah's Story*? Leave a review for this product on guideposts.org/shop. Your feedback helps others in our community find relevant products.

Find inspiration, find faith, find Guideposts.

Shop our best sellers and favorites at

guideposts.org/shop

Or scan the QR code to go directly
to our Shop

Find more inspiring stories in these best-loved Guideposts fiction series!

Mysteries of Lancaster County

Follow the Classen sisters as they unravel clues and uncover hidden secrets in Mysteries of Lancaster County. As you get to know these women and their friends, you'll see how God brings each of them together for a fresh start in life.

Secrets of Wayfarers Inn

Retired schoolteachers find themselves owners of an old warehouse-turned-inn that is filled with hidden passages, buried secrets, and stunning surprises that will set them on a course to puzzling mysteries from the Underground Railroad.

Tearoom Mysteries Series

Mix one stately Victorian home, a charming lakeside town in Maine, and two adventurous cousins with a passion for tea and hospitality. Add a large scoop of intriguing mystery, and sprinkle generously with faith, family, and friends, and you have the recipe for *Tearoom Mysteries*.

Ordinary Women of the Bible

Richly imagined stories—based on facts from the Bible—have all the plot twists and suspense of a great mystery, while bringing you fascinating insights on what it was like to be a woman living in the ancient world.

To learn more about these books, visit Guideposts.org/Shop